SECOND EDITION

SHAPING COLLEGE WRITING

PARAGRAPH AND ESSAY

SECOND EDITION

SHAPING COLLEGE WRITING

PARAGRAPH AND ESSAY

JOSEPH D. GALLO
HENRY W. RINK
FOOTHILL COLLEGE

HARCOURT BRACE JOVANOVICH, INC.

NEW YORK / CHICAGO / SAN FRANCISCO / ATLANTA

ISBN: 0-15-580859-1

Library of Congress Catalog Card Number: 72-93726

Printed in the United States of America

Preface

As a beginning exercise in composition, paragraph writing recommends itself on several counts. The paragraph is the smallest prose unit that lends itself to a close analysis of unity, coherence, and systematic arrangement of thought. If well constructed, it resembles the complete theme in its support of a central idea by means of specifics. Ideally, it is long enough to demand some continuity of thought, yet short enough for the student to grasp as a whole. At its best, it represents an essay in miniature.

As such, the paragraph seems to us to be the best medium for introducing the student to pattern, structure, and arrangement in prose writing without immediately overwhelming him with the complexities of the full-length essay. The beginning student is too often asked to learn as many as twenty new skills at once and, what is more, to perform them all competently. Of course, practicing paragraph writing does not guarantee every student success in all writing skills, but it helps him master the fundamentals of good writing. Teaching the student to make the eventual transition from the paragraph to the essay seems to us more logical than starting with the whole and then, only as a kind of afterthought, considering its parts.

Once the student has developed a firm sense of the structure that underlies a well-organized paragraph, he is ready—we believe—to make the transition to the multiparagraph paper. He has by this time acquired the confidence that comes from learning to impose order on his thoughts. He has discovered that his ideas can be arranged systematically, that there are means of imposing coherence on diverse materials. And as he finds the paragraph increasingly confining, he may also discover that there is more in the world to write about than he had imagined and that he can exert some measure of control over what he finally does choose to treat. Most important, he sees that the difference between a well-structured paragraph and a unifed essay is one of size rather than of kind.

The movement from the most basic unit of paragraph writing to the construction of the whole paragraph is reflected in the order of the chapters in *Shaping College Writing: Paragraph and Essay.* The first chapter stresses the topic sentence with its important controlling idea, which helps the student focus his thoughts and organize his writing around the main idea of the paragraph. Chapters 2 and 3 deal with unity and coherence. Chapter 4 discusses specific sources of support and stresses the student's obligation to check and document the material he uses. Chapter 5 directs the student's attention to the organization of the whole paragraph and introduces the similarities between the paragraph and the essay. In Chapter 6, the student sees the contents of the one-paragraph paper expressed in diagrams that show the rhetorical relationships of its beginning, middle, and end.

Chapter 7 allows the student and instructor to extend the principles of organization and form of a one-paragraph paper to a multiparagraph paper. What we stress in the generalizations governing this extension is that the relationships are the same and the difference is one of scale. A five-paragraph paper is used as the archetype of longer essays, and the student is offered what we hope will be a guide in future writing: the *one-three-nine* structure.

Since this book does not pretend to be a grammar or a reader or a manual on usage, we recommend the use of any supplementary textbooks that the instructor believes are suitable for his course. We feel our book is adaptable to any basic composition course in which emphasis is placed on the principles of structure and concrete support as means of teaching the student to write. To this end exercises have been devised, not to offer the student instant formulas for writing, but rather to help him see structural elements that characterize most well-written prose.

We extend our gratitude to all our colleagues who helped us, joked with us, and encouraged us. But perhaps our greatest debt is to our students at Foothill College, who, over the past ten years, have helped us discover what sorts of pedagogical techniques will work in teaching composition.

Joseph D. Gallo

Henry W. Rink

Contents

SECOND EDITION

SHAPING COLLEGE WRITING

PARAGRAPH AND ESSAY

1
The Topic Sentence

The dominating idea of any paragraph is contained in a key sentence known as the *topic sentence*. This topic sentence—most often found at the beginning of a paragraph—contains the essence of the subject the paragraph deals with. It is, of course, the most important sentence in the paragraph, and it takes the form of a generalization, which is supported or proved by specific facts in the remaining sentences of that paragraph. It may be helpful at this point to examine the difference between a generalization and a specific statement:

A	B
Generalization	Specific Statement
Most women prefer to wear popular clothing styles.	Marnie Ellison wore a plaid kilt and brown suede boots.
Freshmen often find the first week of college confusing.	Fifteen minutes after the bell had rung, a gangling, dark-haired, athletic-looking boy was wandering about the halls asking everyone he met how to get to L-26.
A session in Dr. Malcolm's economics class is a boring experience.	In a voice more soothing than a lullaby, Dr. Malcolm reads page after page of factual information from the old black binder that holds his undergraduate notes.

It is important that the student recognize immediately the difference between the generalization and the specific statement. Note that in column **A** the sentences are broad and nonspecific. They resemble the kinds of sweeping statements we make about the world around us: "Most people are basically dishonest"; or "It usually rains at the beach during spring vacation"; or even an old cliché like "He who laughs last laughs best." The statements in column **B**, on the other hand, focus on specific objects or events. Each could be used to support its companion sentence in column **A**. The specific statements are more concrete—that is, they make reference to individuals (*Marnie Ellison*), patterns and colors (*plaid, brown*), places (*L-26*), time (*fifteen minutes*), articles of clothing (*suede boots*), and physical characteristics (*gangling, dark-haired, athletic-looking*).

Hereafter, generalizations will be used mostly as topic sentences. But to support or develop these generalizations, specific statements are required. Specifics are the substance of writing; a generalization cannot be supported by other generalizations. One looks silly trying to convince thoughtful people that he knows what he's talking about when all he has to offer are vague generalities. For proof of this statement we might glance at a student paragraph that begins with the topic sentence about Dr. Malcolm:

> A session in Dr. Malcolm's economics class is a boring experience. Dr. Malcolm does not know how to liven up a class. He's afraid to do anything exciting or startling. His classes are monotonous and boring for the student. He probably knows a lot about his subject, but his presentation of it leaves much to be desired. His students never get interested in the subject of economics, which should be a pretty great thing to study. As a result, Dr. Malcolm is not a very popular college instructor.

Notice that any one of the sentences in this paragraph could probably be substituted for the topic sentence. Each sentence is a generalization used by the writer in an attempt to support the main idea of the paragraph. As a result, the reader is left wondering what specifically causes Dr. Malcolm's class to be so uninspiring. What do we really know about him after reading the paragraph? Does the man periodically doze at the lectern? Does he turn his back on the class? Has he a speech defect? Is he so bitingly sarcastic toward the class that he becomes tiresome, as most sarcastic people do? Topic sentences like the one above usually cause the reader to ask the question *Why?* It is his right to have that question answered by facts, and it is the writer's obligation to answer the question by providing those facts.

In college writing the approach taken in the sample paragraph above doesn't work, because the writer does not produce facts that convincingly support his topic sentence. Obviously, to be respected in a world where people think, one must be able to bring facts to the defense of one's ideas. Don't be tempted to take the easy way out by writing a paragraph that is only a string of generalizations.

The Controlling Idea

Most workable topic sentences have three distinct parts: subject, verb, and controlling idea. The *subject* is what the sentence is all about; it indicates the general area to be dealt with. The *verb* makes a statement about the subject. The *controlling idea* usually follows these main parts and describes or makes a judgment about the subject, as in the following example:

subj.   *verb*

TS: The poet D. M. Carlson has proved himself a [sensitive observer of nature].

In the above example you can easily see that the subject of the topic sentence is *the poet D. M. Carlson.* A unified paragraph on all a person's attributes (both personal and professional) might run the length of a book. Therefore, the writer must select one aspect of Carlson's personality or career to be developed in the paragraph. The subject is then narrowed in the part of the topic sentence that describes or makes a judgment about the subject—namely, the controlling idea. The main function of the controlling idea, then, is to focus or narrow the subject. Thus, the student using the above example as his topic sentence would deal only with Carlson's sensitive observation of nature. The writer could use examples from certain poems to illustrate his point. However, he must not begin talking about Carlson's private life, his popularity as a poet, his personal peculiarities, his love of fine cars, or the fist fights he's had. Concentrating on the controlling idea prevents such rambling.

True to its name, the controlling idea acts as a controller, or limiter, of what will be discussed in a paragraph. It may be viewed as a contract the writer makes with the reader—a promise to talk only about the portion of the subject that is expressed in the controlling idea. As soon as the writer's supporting sentences stray from the controlling idea, he has broken the contract he made with the reader.

A controlling idea may take several forms. It may be a short phrase, as it is in the example about D. M. Carlson. It may be simply a descriptive word, often an adjective, which explains or limits the subject. Consider the following example:

TS: One can hardly deny that Harley Klentz is a [sloppy dresser].

In this topic sentence the controlling idea is made up of a noun and an adjective describing that noun. In a paragraph about Harley Klentz, the writer would develop the idea of the descriptive word *sloppy* as it applied to Klentz's various garments.

Often the controlling idea is a single descriptive word:

TS: Most of his friends agree that Brumley Sinkwich is [generous].

When the controlling idea is a descriptive word, as it is in the above sentence, it is helpful if you define it, especially if it isn't a commonly used term. Of course, we know what *generous* means, but if the word you choose happens to be *magnanimous* or *eccentric,* you may need to look it up in a dictionary to be sure of its meaning. After all, it would be embarrassing to find, upon checking the dictionary, that your paragraph had nothing to do with the actual meaning of the controlling idea.

It is important that you recognize what your controlling idea is and that the controlling idea be limited and readily defined. It may also be helpful if you position the controlling idea near the end of the topic sentence so that it is the last thing the reader sees before getting to the supporting information. The following examples illustrate how topic sentences that attempt to cover too broad an area can be improved by limiting the controlling idea:

3

Rudimentary Topic Sentence	Revision
Cerebros College has a beautiful campus.	The landscaping at Cerebros College makes attractive use of symmetrical groups of shade trees.

Obviously, *symmetrical* is much more readily defined than *beautiful,* a term that both philosophers and English instructors have been haggling over for centuries. Notice also that in the revision the area under discussion is reduced from an entire campus—which couldn't be covered adequately even in a twenty-page essay, let alone a paragraph—to one attractive feature of that campus, the positioning and arrangement of the shade trees. Let's try another example:

Rudimentary Topic Sentence	Revision
Cerebros College has many interesting features.	Visitors to Cerebros College have described the architecture of the library as modified Oriental.

Interesting is the sort of adjective one uses to describe a modern painting that he doesn't understand but is too embarrassed to criticize; it's a vague word that gets a person off the hook without committing himself. *Modified Oriental,* on the other hand, gives us a mental picture of the building being described. Again, notice that we have decreased the scope of our description from *many interesting features* to the architectural style of one particular building, *the library.* Doesn't it seem more effective to describe a single specific feature than to allude to countless unspecified ones? In light of this, consider the following example:

Rudimentary Topic Sentence	Revision
The area by the Cerebros library is a really neat place.	During the warm months the quad in front of the Cerebros library is a showplace for contemporary clothing styles.

Neat is a word used by elderly women to describe an orderly room, by drinkers to denote straight whiskey, and by teen-age girls to describe their current idols. Any term that can be readily applied to so many situations should be rejected by the student who wishes to write with precision. The revision gets down to specifics: the vague *area* becomes *quad*; the quad isn't simply *by* the library, it is *in front* of it; and we know what the writer had in mind when he used the term *neat*—the clothing worn by the students.

As you have perhaps noticed in the above examples, the writer was able to improve each topic sentence, to make it more workable, by choosing his controlling idea and by positioning it near the end of his topic sentence. Now let's try to duplicate the actual process of creating and refining a topic sentence with its controlling idea.

Suppose you lived near a road to an abandoned quarry where motorcyclists liked to race and to climb slopes with their bikes. Every day you looked down at the riders roaring by, wearing leather jackets or sleeveless ponchos, revving their motors, sometimes discarding their empty beer cans along the roadside. Occasionally, you'd see the

4

police arrive in response to some neighbor's call. The cyclists would disperse, but as soon as the policemen left, they would return to resume their sport. Eventually, annoyed by the repeated disturbances, you might conclude that people who ride motorcycles are a pretty loud and undesirable group. The process used in arriving at this conclusion is the same as the one by which topic sentences (and opinions and arguments) are made.

Now suppose you were to put that raw inference down in the form of a topic sentence:

Motorcyclists are pretty bad citizens.

Many students might choose such a sentence, and, what is more, try to support it. But most first attempts can usually be improved. There is too much wrong with this sentence for it to be of value to you in writing a good paragraph. First, the adjective *bad* has countless applications, even in a small dictionary. Any term that can be as loosely applied to almost any undesirable situation is a poor prospect for a controlling idea. Second, a man's creating a public disturbance doesn't necessarily indicate that he's "bad." Many law-abiding citizens sometimes disturb others with their activities—noisy parties, for instance. According to the topic sentence, however, you have committed yourself to proving that motorcyclists are bad citizens. Obviously, you aren't likely to prove such a generalization, certainly not in one paragraph.

What might be a more valid proposition that you could develop about motorcyclists? Suppose you tried to restrict your proposition a little, to draw it into a more provable assertion. Perhaps you begin to think about the *reasons* for the riders' behavior, and you conclude that most of their actions are defensive in nature. So you try a new topic sentence:

Motorcyclists reveal their defensiveness by their public conduct.

This may be a little better, but it's still too big and a little vague as well. True, you could summarize the types of illegal conduct you have observed: the discarding of empty beer cans along the roadside, the removal of mufflers to give the bikes more hill-climbing power, the destruction of grass and ground cover by bike tires. You can certainly observe the *effects* of the riders' activities. You can also note the *physical causes* of these effects. But can you really perceive the *psychological causes* of the riders' conduct? You are only assuming that these acts reveal defensiveness; perhaps they simply indicate high spirits or a disregard for public opinion or public peace. Then too, not *all* motorcyclists behave loudly and destructively. The topic sentence is obviously too sweeping a generalization. You must try a different approach to the subject.

Perhaps you remember something your brother once mentioned about his own motorcycling activities. "With my machine under me," he said, "I feel I can do anything. My buddies feel the same way." On another occasion, when you asked him why he didn't just sell his chronically broken motorcycle, he said, "If I did that, there'd be nothing but me. And man, that's not enough!" From an article by Dr. Martin Milobar in *Psychology Today* magazine, you jot down a quotation: "Victims of the motorcycle syndrome often experience a full-time preoccupation with the machine. Unlike the healthy

5

cyclist, the compulsive rider feels diminished when he is even temporarily without his bike." When you question one of your brother's friends, he tells you, "The noise, you know? When you move in on a girl with your bike, it feels right." Now you begin to generate a more confident theory about *certain* motorcyclists:

> Compulsive motorcyclists reveal their lack of personal confidence in several ways.

or

> My brother Niccolo's sense of personal inadequacy is shown by his feelings about his motorcycle.

You have evidence—quoted testimony from motorcyclists themselves and a statement by a psychiatrist—to substantiate your theory. No doubt you could find other material to support your topic sentence, which has now been narrowed down to a compact generalization—limited and definable. The process of creating your topic sentence took time. Along the way you had to reject certain notions and try to devise more sensible alternatives. But you will probably be happier with your third attempt than you would have been trying to support your first one.

The process of supporting the topic sentence through specific facts is taken up in Chapter 4. Here we are concerned mostly with the controlling idea of the topic sentence and with whether that controlling idea can be supported within a single, unified paragraph. If you can't devise a topic sentence with a clearly defined controlling idea, chances are you can't produce a successful paragraph. Few paragraphs survive a poor topic sentence. Let's look at some workable topic sentences with their controlling ideas (descriptive parts) underlined and then defined:

1. For being chosen Man of the Year, Miniver Winlocke received several <u>appropriate</u> awards.
   appropriate   suitable, fitting, proper, suited to the honor or situation.
2. The typical guerrilla is an <u>efficient</u> ground fighter.
   efficient   working well, competent, producing the desired effect or result with the minimum effort.
3. Professor Pontoon can always be counted on to deliver a <u>disorderly</u> lecture.
   disorderly   messy, riotous, untidy, unsystematic, unruly.
4. When the going is hard, Al Prufrock usually sets a <u>cowardly</u> example.
   cowardly   having or showing lack of courage, extremely timid.

This list should give the student an idea of the sort of topic sentence that has a chance of working in a well-controlled paragraph. Observe how each controlling idea points toward the facts that will be used to support it. In the first sentence, for instance, the reader will expect the writer to identify the awards by name and description. The writer of the second topic sentence will have to list precisely those traits that make the guerrilla an efficient soldier. In the third sentence the reader will want to know exactly what ingredients go into the production of Pontoon's disorderly lecture. In other words, the topic sentence points to the kind of facts that will be used in its own support. Notice also that the controlling idea is usually placed close to the end of the sentence. Strategically speaking, the controlling idea might well be the last thing the reader sees before he gets into the support itself.

One other characteristic of most good topic sentences should be noted—their *brevity*. It is a valuable rule of thumb for the writer to keep his topic sentences short. Of course, to write a long, sophisticated sentence isn't against any law. But the chances of the writer's becoming confused and not supporting the most important part of the topic sentence are great when the statement is wordy and involved. Consider the following perfectly workable topic sentence:

> Although only fifteen years old and the youngest member of a generally youthful and brilliant graduating class, Melvin Balloon has already invented several labor-saving household devices.

The writer who devises such a sentence runs the risk of focusing on the fact that Melvin is young or that his class is youthful or even that his class is brilliant. Perhaps all these considerations have their place in the paragraph. But the important point is that brilliant, young Melvin has invented several labor-saving devices; that's the point that needs to be supported. That's also the point that could get lost in this sentence. And if the writer simply can't resist the urge to create long topic sentences, he should at least remember to place the main idea in the main, or independent, clause.

A more urgent warning can be delivered about topic sentences that are likely to be losers from the start. Avoid what is sometimes called the dead-end topic sentence, one that either lacks a controlling idea or else fails to point in any direction at all:

1. The library is filled with books.
2. This campus has a total of 1,107 classrooms.
3. In 1492 Columbus discovered the New World.
4. China has a large population.

None of the above statements lends itself to unified paragraph structure. None of them points toward any concise group of facts that could support it. Each lacks a controlling idea and tends to be too factual to act as a supportable generalization.

The wild guess is another kind of topic sentence that the writer should avoid. Note the following:

1. When I graduate from college, it shouldn't take me more than five years to own two cars and to move into a good neighborhood.
2. Most of the students in this class will probably settle in this area after graduation.

You must admit that it is difficult to find facts to support these generalizations. No facts exist, of course, that will reveal precisely what will happen next year. Only an expert can make an educated guess about the future on the basis of present trends. Remember, you are a writer, not a fortuneteller.

Finally, it is a good policy to avoid posing a question as a topic sentence:

1. What is the significance of today's dance trends?
2. How can one write a good paper?

How indeed? One could ramble on and on about such subjects. Assert yourself! Know what you're writing about. Don't be tentative or questioning when you have facts to support a statement. Make the topic sentence a statement, not a cry for help.

Summary: Topic Sentence and Controlling Idea

1. The topic sentence contains the dominating idea that will be developed in the paragraph.
2. The topic sentence is the writer's promise to the reader to deliver factual support.
3. The topic sentence should be placed at the beginning of the paragraph. It is easier to form a paragraph from a key idea than to lead up to that idea.
4. The controlling idea is the essential part of the topic sentence.
5. The controlling idea is a word or phrase that is limited and readily defined.
6. The controlling idea is best placed toward the end of the topic sentence.
7. Although a topic sentence may contain more than one clause, it is best to keep the sentence short and concise.
8. If the writer chooses a complex topic sentence, the controlling idea should appear in the main clause. (Clauses will be discussed at greater length in the next chapter.)
9. Avoid the dead-end topic sentence, which lacks a controlling idea and points in no direction whatsoever.
10. Avoid the question and the prediction as topic sentences.

Writing a good topic sentence takes time and practice. The writer must often discard several prospective sentences before narrowing down his final product to a workable unit. But achieving a good topic sentence is essential and worth the effort involved. For though it wouldn't be true to say that a good topic sentence unconditionally guarantees a successful paragraph, without one you might just as well file your notebook and go out to see a movie instead.

EXERCISE 1: *In the blank at the left, write G if the sentence is a generalization and S if it is specific.*

____ 1. In Vietnam, the U.S. Army once used a defoliant known as "agent orange."
____ 2. Besides killing vegetation, "agent orange" is known to have some startling side effects on the environment.
____ 3. Doctors' fees in the United States have risen 22 percent since 1967.
____ 4. The President's Committee on Mental Retardation estimates that 3 percent of the population under age 65 suffers some degree of mental retardation.

_9_ 5. Many cases of mental retardation among children could be prevented by
the intelligent application of present knowledge.
_3_ 6. The Hopi Indians believe that the San Francisco peaks of northern Arizona
are the home of the *kachinas,* the spiritual forces of the universe.
_9_ 7. According to the Hopis, the *kachinas* have some very important agricultural
functions.
_3_ 8. Daniel Ellsberg, a former Pentagon consultant, is the man who released to
the *New York Times* certain top-secret documents that revealed United
States policy in Vietnam in the 1960's.
_9_ 9. The release to the public of the Pentagon documents threw the press and
the government into a bitter legal conflict, which still lingers today.
_9_ 10. In conducting its case against Lloyd Bucher, commander of the *U.S.S.
Pueblo,* the U.S. Navy tried in every way possible to prove Bucher guilty.
_3_ 11. *The Immense Journey* by Loren Eiseley contains thirteen essays dealing
with "the mysteries of man and nature."
_5_ 12. On Labor Day in 1963 Mario Andretti won seven midget-car races—three
in the afternoon in Flemington, New Jersey, and four that night in Hatfield,
Pennsylvania.

EXERCISE 2: *The aim of this exercise is to clarify the distinction between a generalization and a specific. For each of the following sentences, supply one
or two specific facts that support the generalization.*

Example: Men's styles of dress and personal grooming are much less conservative than
they were ten years ago.
fact: Many men now have shoulder-length hair.
fact: Today colored shirts, wide ties, and flared trousers are in fashion.

1. Muhammad Ali has been called the most controversial sports figure of the last
twenty-five years.

fact: _Ali writes poetry_
fact: _His real name is Cassius Clay_

2. The Vietnam war has had disturbing repercussions at home.

fact: _It caused many student protests_
fact: _All the young men are gone_

3. The instructor of this class has certain mannerisms that draw the students' attention
to him.

fact: _A smile on his face_
fact: _Eye to eye contact_

9

4. Many of today's rock groups are pretty unconventional in their physical appearance.

fact: _Alice Cooper wears lots of eye makeup_

fact: _Most costumes cost approx. $1000_ (elaborate)

5. The person who sits in front of me is dressed in conventional, collegiate clothing.

fact: _She is wearing jeans._

fact: _She is well groomed_

6. Attending college is expensive.

fact: _I just shelled out ^980 for 1 semester_

fact: _The college has many expenses_

7. The young man who has long hair occasionally runs into difficulties in public.

fact: _Police will pull him over more readily_

fact: _He is stereotyped._

8. This college sponsors a number of student activities.

fact: _They have a student gov. body_

fact: _They have varied sports_

9. The requirements of this course have been spelled out in detail in the syllabus.

fact: _Freshman English must be passed_

fact: _A score of 80 is required to pass the_ (grammar test)

10. There are certain kinds of part-time jobs that are available to anyone who wants to do them.

fact: _McDonalds always needs people._

fact: _They don't pay well_

EXERCISE 3: *In each of the following topic sentences, underline the word or phrase that represents the controlling idea. Remember that the controlling idea is the specific element of the topic sentence that will be developed in the paragraph.*

1. As far as many parents are concerned, the growth in popularity of the motorcycle has gotten out of hand.
2. In this country, the motorcycle craze has created a lucrative business.
3. Oil and politics have always been a volatile mixture.

4. According to a Denver psychologist, actor James Stewart projects one of middle-class America's most admired images.
5. Soviet cosmonauts discovered that extended exposure to a lack of gravity impairs certain physiological functions.
6. Ralph Nader's recent investigation of nursing homes revealed that medical procedures in these establishments are often slipshod.
7. Over the years, U.S. policy toward Latin America has been inconsistent.
8. According to conservationists, snowmobiles are a threat to the environment.
9. The National Commission on Marijuana and Drug Abuse has called the idea that pot-smoking leads to heroin use "totally invalid."
10. As a general recreational vehicle, the pickup truck offers some obvious advantages over the automobile and the van.

EXERCISE 4: *Many of the following topic sentences are either dead-end or lacking in direction. Choose the one from each group that seems best suited for development into a paragraph. Look for the sentence that narrows down to a workable idea and underline that idea. Then try to develop a paragraph from each sentence you have chosen.*

1. a. Thomas Berger's novel *Little Big Man* was made into a great movie.
   b. Several scenes in the movie that began dramatically ended comically.
   c. Dustin Hoffman played the lead role in the movie.
2. a. The fact that President Nixon telephoned Billy Jean King to congratulate her on on being the first woman tennis player to win $100,000 in a single year shows his enthusiasm for winners.
   b. The President's phone call to Billy Jean King shows that he is really a nice guy.
   c. The phone call is an example of the President's interest in athletic prowess.
3. a. Because of its hardness and resistance to splitting, the wood from elm trees has many industrial uses.
   b. Elm trees are very valuable.
   c. Elm wood is used for pulley blocks.
4. a. In a downtown hotel last night, a woman gave metropolitan police their fiercest battle of the year.
   b. A 24-year-old, 72-pound, 4-foot 4-inch woman was apprehended by police last night.
   c. A small, disreputable downtown hotel was the scene of a hassle.
5. a. Hermann Hesse was a great German writer.
   b. Hesse received the Nobel Prize for literature in 1946.
   c. In *Narcissus and Goldmund* Hesse attempts to bring into harmony asceticism and estheticism, two poles of human nature.
6. a. Because of racial discrimination, Satchel Paige did not pitch in major league baseball until he had reached the age at which most other pitchers retire.
   b. In 1971, Mayor Wheeler of Kansas City proclaimed October 3 "Satchel Paige Day" and gave Paige the keys to the city.
   c. Satchel Paige's story is similar to that of many other black athletes in the United States.

7. a. Composers of classical music generally live in a dream world of their own.
   b. Events in the short, difficult life of Franz Schubert reflect his great dedication to music.
   c. Schubert, who lived in Austria, was a great composer of the early nineteenth century.
8. a. Four days before Christmas in 1951, 119 miners died in a coal mine explosion in West Frankfort, Illinois.
   b. America's coal mines have a higher accident rate than those of any other industrial nation.
   c. The accident rate in American mines is about six times as high as it is in Holland.
   d. In his book *Betrayal in the Mines,* Harry M. Caudill says that "Virtually every lump of coal is paid for with human blood and agony."
9. a. Coal is the greatest single source of power in the United States, supplying about half the nation's needs.
   b. Coal is valuable stuff.
   c. One of the most interesting facts about coal is that it has a wide range of uses.
10. a. Ginseng is a root.
    b. Ginseng is good for you.
    c. Ginseng has valuable medicinal properties.
    d. Chinese people like ginseng.
11. a. Christmas in Italy is a merry time of the year.
    b. On Christmas Eve the people of the Italian town of Santa Cristina observe several well-known customs.
    c. There's no one like Italians when it comes to Christmas.

EXERCISE 5: *Do exactly as you did in the preceding exercise.*

1. a. "Adjusting to the realities of life" usually means compromising whatever ideals and principles we had when we were young.
   b. Young guys are better than old guys.
   c. No one past twelve can be trusted.
2. a. The tuna may become extinct.
   b. The tuna is being destroyed by man's greed.
   c. The tuna's survival is threatened by modern fishing methods.
3. a. If Japanese and Russian fishing fleets just went home, there would be plenty of fish for everybody.
   b. The problem of dwindling supplies of fish could be solved easily by a few simple changes in territorial water laws.
   c. Fish are too stupid to survive.
4. a. The death penalty should be abolished.
   b. The death penalty is barbarous.
   c. The death penalty in the United States discriminates against racial minorities and the poor.
5. a. Christopher Columbus, whose real name was Cristoforo Colombo, discovered the West Indies in 1492.

12

b. Before his departure from Spain, Christopher Columbus experienced some discouraging legal setbacks.

c. Columbus was not a Spaniard, but rather an Italian who sailed under the Spanish flag.

6. a. Gabriel García Márquez is an exceptionally gifted Colombian writer.

b. In reading his novel *One Hundred Years of Solitude,* one is reminded of the writings of Rabelais, Faulkner, and Sterne.

c. His novel should be around for a long time.

7. a. Of all professional football players, the members of "suicide" squads run the greatest risk of injury.

b. Professional football players really take a beating.

c. Players on the special, or "suicide," squads are really weird guys.

8. a. Alexandria, Egypt, is named after Alexander the Great.

b. A famous meeting between Alexander the Great and Diogenes, a poor Greek philosopher who is said to have worn a barrel, is described in a humorous anecdote.

c. Alexander the Great died in 323 B.C.

9. a. On April 10, 1912, the *Titanic* left Southampton for New York.

b. The *Titanic,* nicknamed "The Millionaire's Special," was luxuriously outfitted.

c. The disastrous trip was the *Titanic*'s maiden voyage.

10. a. Irving Bedrock always has a gallon of burgundy in his car.

b. Bedrock carries a notebook containing the names of every girl he's ever known and some he's never met.

c. Irving Bedrock may well be the most aggressive male in New York.

EXERCISE 6: *Here we are to some extent reversing the process. This exercise provides you with a group of specific facts that have something in common. Your task is to determine the subject of that group of facts. Place it in the first blank. Then choose a descriptive word or short phrase that makes a judgment or statement about the subject. Check a dictionary to be sure that the word or phrase that you have chosen as the controlling idea is accurate. Place it in the second blank and then give a definition of it in the third blank.*

Example: a. Two years ago, when in college, Bilkstaff earned $14,000 per year with his research-paper service.

b. Three months after graduation he purchased the major stock in Bumble Billiard Company, a million-dollar-a-year enterprise.

c. Soon afterward he headed the Coleman Cookie Company, a major midwestern corporation.

d. Last year the Coleman Cookie Company merged with the Remington Jelly Company, a consolidation worth several million dollars.

e. At the beginning of this fiscal year Bilkstaff owned four major companies, and was earning an estimated $3 million yearly.

Subj.: *Bilkstaff's rise to fortune*   CI: *meteoric*

Definition of CI: *like a meteor; dazzling or brilliant; flashing or swift.*

1. a. Lily Parsell married a home town banker at the age of twenty-two.
   b. Divorced at twenty-four, she soon married a congressman.
   c. At twenty-eight she was widowed; she then married the heir to the Borax fortune.
   d. Ten years later she wed a Panamanian playboy.
   e. She recently became engaged to a West German diplomat.

Subj.: _____   CI: _____

Definition of CI: _____

_____

2. a. Vojislav Stefanovic fought for the Serbian partisans in 1943.
   b. Stefanovic was imprisoned by the Tito government from 1949 to 1951 for subversive political activities.
   c. From 1955 to 1957 he was a Soviet agent in Albania.
   d. He defected to the West from Austria in 1959.
   e. He worked for British counterintelligence in the Balkans from 1961 to 1963.
   f. He was indicted by the British for selling rocket specifications in Sofia, Bulgaria.
   g. He was traded to the Russians for a captured British agent.
   h. Stefanovic was last seen in Budapest in 1966.

Subj.: _____   CI: _____

Definition of CI: _____

_____

3. a. On summer nights the windows of Kensey Brundle's old house glow with blue light.
   b. People have seen dark figures prowling about the grounds on rainy nights.
   c. Sounds of distant growling and crying come from the house during winter.
   d. Tracks of an enormous pair of hobnailed shoes were found there after heavy snows.
   e. During the summer, smoke sometimes rises from the chimney.

Subj.: _____   CI: _____

Definition of CI: _____

_____

4. a. Milton E. Grundy, chairman of the board of Broadwhistle Industries, often shouts at subordinates, "Don't feel! Think! Thinking's what produces corporate assets."

b. Grundy often awakens subordinates at 3:00 A.M. for facts missing from reports submitted.

c. He once screamed at a junior executive, "You can't find your feet with both hands!"

d. He expects executives to have all pertinent statistics completely memorized when they talk to him.

e. All subordinates are required to stand in his presence.

Subj.: _____ CI: _____

Definition of CI: _____

_____

5. a. Winston Kegbeer cooks excellent shish kebab for his friends.

b. He built his own home on land that he purchased with his earnings as a postman.

c. He flies a Cessna to Santa Rosa on weekends.

d. He builds furniture from walnut and maple and paints fine pictures with water colors.

e. He restores antique cars to perfect condition.

Subj.: _____ CI: _____

Definition of CI: _____

_____

6. a. After a fight with Pacific Utilities over her electric bill, Mrs. Amelia Palooka closed her account and has used kerosene lamps ever since.

b. Mrs. Palooka always tells her son Fester, "If you want something done right, do it yourself."

c. She grows and cans enough fruits and vegetables to keep her pantry stocked all year round.

d. When the city refused to remove a huge pile of debris that the rain had washed onto her property, Mrs. Palooka rented a bulldozer and removed it herself.

e. She makes all her own clothing.

Subj.: _____ CI: _____

Definition of CI: _____

_____

7. a. At the age of twelve Finley Ordway was beaten up by his teammates for selling his football team's secret plays to the opponents for a buck.

b. In his junior year of high school he ran naked across the stage of the auditorium during an assembly to win a dollar bet.

c. At fifteen he attempted to strangle his 102-year-old great-aunt Faith Ordway because she wouldn't tell him where she had hidden her purse.

d. At twenty he was fired from his job at Major Motors for selling the plans of a cotter pin for a buck.

e. Ten years later he was picked up by the border patrol while trying to peddle "We Love Nixon" buttons to Mexican soldiers—for a buck.

Subj.: _____ CI: _____

Definition of CI: _____

_____

8. a. Kate is a member of one of the fiercest factions of the Irish Republican Army in Belfast.

b. Her favorite weapon is a Thompson submachine gun.

c. She says she is willing to do anything to defeat the enemy—blow them up, shoot them, anything at all.

d. She constantly risks imprisonment and death in her gunrunning and in her attempts to lure British troops and police to their deaths.

e. She is pretty, well educated, and used to have a good job.

f. Her boyfriend is in prison, serving a long term for gunrunning.

Subj.: _____ CI: _____

Definition of CI: _____

_____

9. a. In industrialized countries millions of people trade in automobiles and appliances long before they are worn out.

b. In addition, every day they destroy countless tons of containers—bags, boxes, bottles, and cans—that are still in usable condition.

c. Girls may now trade in their old Barbie dolls for new models.

d. Many clothing stores are featuring disposable clothes.

e. One company is now manufacturing disposable wedding gowns. Their advertisement states that the gowns will make "great kitchen curtains after the ceremony."

Subj.: _____ CI: _____

Definition of CI: _____

_____

10. a. Mrs. Lucille Loury oversees most of the bookkeeping for her husband's highly successful pharmacy chain.

b. She is the den mother of her son's Cub Scout pack and a state adviser for the Girl Scouts.

c. Mrs. Loury devotes two mornings a week to charity work at nearby St. Jude's Hospital.

d. Three evenings a week, she lectures on fiction-writing techniques at the local college.
e. Under the pen name of Agnes Davalle, she has written five best-selling mystery novels.

Subj.: _____ CI: _____

Definition of CI: _____

_____

11. a. As a young soldier in the Second World War, the Russian novelist Alexander Solzhenitsyn was seriously wounded, but he survived the five years of warfare against the Germans.
b. At the end of the war he was sent to a Siberian prison camp for criticizing Stalin in a letter to a friend.
c. He endured eight terrible years in the prison labor camp and another three years in exile.
d. In the 1950's he was hospitalized and treated for cancer. After his return to western Russia he began teaching math in high school and writing books protesting the harsh treatment of dissidents in Soviet Russia.
e. Of his numerous books, only *One Day in the Life of Ivan Denisovich* has been published in Russia. But Solzhenitsyn continues to write, and his books are published in translations outside of Russia.
f. In 1970 he received the Nobel Prize for literature, but he was told by the Soviet government that if he went to Sweden to receive the prize, he would not be allowed to return. Despite the various forms of persecution he has been subjected to, he chose to remain in Russia and continue to write the truth as he sees it.

Subj.: _____ CI: _____

Definition of CI: _____

_____

12. a. Of the top ten cigarette brands, only Pall Mall's sales remained stable between 1956 and 1966. Camels and Lucky Strikes lost 50 percent of their sales; Salem's sales, however, multiplied nine times.
b. In the last fifteen years it has become increasingly common for a customer to discover that a brand he has used and wants to buy again is no longer on the market.
c. In 1966, 7,000 new products appeared for sale. In 1968, in the packaged-goods field alone, 9,500 new products made their debut. However, only one out of five of these met its sales target, and many of the others were dropped from production. Fifty-five percent of the products now available to the American consumer were not in existence ten years ago, and thousands will be dropped by the commercial wayside, only to be replaced by similar products bearing different brand names.

d. Economist Robert Theobald has said that items that once would have remained on the market for twenty-five years are now likely to last only five. Pharmaceutical and electronic products may change every six months or so.

Subj.: _____ CI: _____

Definition of CI: _____

_____

EXERCISE 7: *Do exactly as you did in the preceding exercise.*

1. a. Twelve-year-old Ginny Greatheart spends most of her days at Pepperwood Junior High gazing at her classmate Mike Mettle.
   b. He has spoken to her only once—to bawl her out for being out of step in band marching practice.
   c. She has spoken to him only once—to say, "Shut up, Big Mouth Mike Mettle!"
   d. At home, between fantasies about Bobby Sherman, David Cassidy, and Donny Osmond, she spends most of her time sighing over and talking about Mike Mettle.
   e. She has made "Mike Mettle" posters and put them up all around her room. They read: "Peace and love, Mike Mettle"; "I think I love you, Mike Mettle"; "I know I love you, Mike Mettle"; "Merry Christmas, Mike Mettle"; and "Be my valentine, Mike Mettle."
   f. Her father finally asked her, "Why don't you tell him you love him?"
   g. Ginny answered, "Daddy, are you crazy?"

Subj.: _____ CI: _____

Definition of CI: _____

_____

2. a. In most American prisons inmates all but lose their names and become known mainly as numbers.
   b. Their personal possessions are taken from them.
   c. They are all forced to dress in the same dull uniforms.
   d. They must be cleanshaven, and their hair is either crew cut or completely shaved.
   e. The prison walls are almost always painted battleship gray.
   f. The prisoner is not permitted to have anything in his cell or on his person that is distinctive or individual.

Subj.: _____ CI: _____

Definition of CI: _____

_____

3. a. RAF Lieutenant Peter Wingate flew in the Battle of Britain in 1940.
   b. Captain Wingate was shot down in North Africa in 1942.
   c. Group Commander Wingate was shot down over Palermo in 1943.
   d. He was then rescued by partisans.
   e. After the war he was one of the few survivors of the *Andrea Doria* Disaster.

Subj.: _____ CI: _____

Definition of CI: _____

_____

4. a. Ronald Rooter buys double-knit shirts from Roos-Atkins.
   b. He buys Italian-made leather boots.
   c. He is partial to flamboyant neckties.
   d. His suits and slacks are carefully tailored in the latest styles.
   e. In cold weather he sports a fleece-lined car coat from Norway.

Subj.: _____ CI: _____

Definition of CI: _____

_____

5. a. The typical Hemingway hero is a man who is physically and intellectually
      wounded.
   b. He does not gripe or try to make excuses for himself.
   c. He is a man of few words.
   d. He tries to "hold tight" and avoid crying out when in danger.
   e. When he is in trouble, he doesn't tell anybody.

Subj.: _____ CI: _____

Definition of CI: _____

_____

6. a. Bernard Branchforth has long hair and a beard, which he has trimmed twice a
      month by an expensive hair stylist.
   b. He drives a late-model Pontiac with mags and slicks.
   c. He has several novels by Hesse, collections of Borges' stories and essays, a book
      of poetry by James Dickey, a paperback collection of poetry of the Western
      world, and two books on yoga. He has never read any of these books, and he
      doesn't know the difference between yoga and yogurt.
   d. A month ago, he bought a $165 suede coat at an exclusive store. He slept in it
      for two weeks, ran over it with his car several times, and applied three patches to
      it to make it look old.
   e. He enrolled in a journalism class at Excelsior Junior College, and he now tells
      everyone he's majoring in humanities at college.

Subj.: _____ CI: _____

Definition of CI: _____

_____

7. a. In a recent speech, college instructor Benjamin Pumpernickel told a women's
      club that their organization was one of the symbols of "emasculated America."
   b. He always greets new classes with the statement, "Intellectually, most of you
      were ambushed in the nursery."
   c. He told the dean that the college dress code was "juvenile and degrading."
   d. He characterized two-year colleges as "high schools with ashtrays."
   e. He wrote to the state legislature demanding that the governor be impeached.

Subj.: _____ CI: _____

Definition of CI: _____

_____

8. a. Al Blunt's favorite number is seven.
   b. He never steps on a crack in the pavement.
   c. He carries a rabbit's foot.
   d. He never does anything an even number of times.

Subj.: _____ CI: _____

Definition of CI: _____

_____

9. a. In Professor Muller's class there are usually three students talking audibly during
      the lecture.
   b. Halfway through the lecture a boy enters and drags a projector across the room.
   c. A man in the last row incessantly drums on his desk with a pencil.
   d. Muller often changes the subject abruptly or else has a three-minute coughing fit.
   e. Sometimes during a lecture the professor simply stares into space for five min-
      utes at a time.

Subj.: _____ CI: _____

Definition of CI: _____

_____

10. a. Paul Pinchwick speaks admiringly of his friends.
    b. He gives credit to whoever else has helped with a project.
    c. Last spring he refused to admit that he had been helping a poor family financially.
    d. He recently forgave two teenagers who completely wrecked his prize greenhouse.
    e. He said, "Pressing charges won't restore my greenhouse, but it could hurt them
       in the future."

Subj.: _____ CI: _____

Definition of CI: _____

_____

You may have noticed that in extracting subjects and controlling ideas from each list of facts in the last two exercises, you have been using a certain method of reasoning. In all likelihood, what you were doing was moving from the particular to the general, or, in other words, moving from specific data to a conclusion, or from the smaller to the larger. This is called *inductive reasoning.* From a mass of details, you induct, or infer, an idea, generalization, or conclusion that the details all seem to be leading to. For example, if on first meeting you, a certain girl ignores you, then at the next meeting forgets your name, and on the third meeting seems openly antagonistic, it's probably not a good idea to call her up for a date. That's the conclusion the individual facts lead up to.

In the following exercise you will continue to use inductive reasoning, except that your conclusion (point, big idea, generalization) will be expressed more completely and more formally in a topic sentence. You will also notice that some of the sets of facts will lead to only one rationally possible topic sentence, while others will allow several different interpretations or topic sentences.

We often hear people say, "All that can mean only one thing" or, "That leads to only one conclusion." Hasn't it seemed to you that much of the time people find only the answers or conclusions they *want* to find and that they refuse to interpret facts or data in a manner that will lead to a conclusion they don't like? In formulating topic sentences in the following exercise, try to see if, in some cases, two or three others might work equally well.

EXERCISE 8: *Devise one or more topic sentences to accommodate each set of facts listed below. Be sure that the controlling idea is the logical summation of the facts given and that it accounts for all the facts.*

1. a. Pulitzer Prize-winning poet Richard Kingsley Richard worked for twenty-two years before one of his poems was published in a major magazine.
   b. During the summer of 1939, Richard had to subsist on string beans, zucchini, and beets that he grew along a creek and watered with a bucket fashioned from a discarded five-gallon oil can.
   c. He served in the infantry from 1942 to 1945 and wrote poetry on toilet paper, using his helmet as a desk during lulls in the battles of Anzio and Monte Cassino.
   d. From 1946 to 1949 Richard worked as a hod-carrier in California and wrote poetry at night and on weekends.
   e. In 1950, when his fiancée died of tuberculosis, Richard had a nervous breakdown and was confined to the state hospital for a year. It was while he was recovering that he wrote the *Penitentia Creek Anthology*, which was to bring him fame and some money to live on.
   f. A critic recently said of his poem "Night Places" that "like all of Richard's work, it is hammered with honesty out of the agony of near-defeat."

21

2. a. "Little Moses" George Breckinridge, 7 foot 11 inch rookie center for the Parkhill Playboys basketball team, scored 56 points in his first professional game against the Johnstown Jawbones.
   b. Ten games later his average was 86 points a game, and he had led the Playboys to a ten-game winning streak.
   c. With ten minutes to go in a game against the Riverport Ripples, he fouled out for sitting on Ripple forward Bennie Butts as Butts attempted to dribble between Little Moses' legs. At that moment the Playboys were leading 98 to 64. Without Little Moses they lost the game 103 to 99.
   d. In the next game, against the Butchertown Butchers, brawny Butcher guard Dutch Gottschlaub smacked "Little Moses" in the solar plexus in the opening minutes of the game. Playboy coach "Lemon-Head" Bernstein, wildly protesting, said he saw the punch "all the way."
   e. In each of the next four games similar attempts were made on the life of Little Moses. Though he was never quite killed, he was carried off the floor each time, and the Playboys always lost by a wide margin.
   f. After the American Basketball Club wrote new rules to protect players against mayhem, "Little Moses" went on to lead his team to their first ABC championship.

3. a. According to Euell Gibbon, stinging nettle—which grows wild along creeks and in swamps—is extremely nourishing when boiled and eaten salted, like spinach or chard.
   b. Free-growing cactus pears, or prickly pears, have long been a nutritional source of sweets for Mexican-Americans in the Southwest and people living on the southern shores of the Mediterranean.
   c. The piñon nut, the fruit of the wild piñon tree of northern Mexico and the southwestern United States, has more protein value than beefsteak.
   d. Young mustard leaves, which grow on hillsides, are said to be one of the greatest sources of oxalic acid, which is required in a well-rounded diet.

4. a. In the late nineteenth century, British prisoners began to grow sickly after coarse, whole-grain breads were replaced by white-flour bread as the staple of their diet.
   b. In many isolated, so-called backward parts of the world, whole-grain breads and cereals are among the chief dietary staples. Generally the people of these regions are in excellent health and live to remarkably old ages without the aid of vitamin pills, tonics, geriatric medicines, or other such dietary supplements.
   c. During the Second World War, Russian soldiers and civilians alike became famous for their ability to withstand the effects of strenuous labor and exposure to extreme cold. Black bread made from whole-grain flour was one of the staples of their diet and often their only food.
   d. In the United States more and more scientists and nutritionists are beginning to recognize the superiority of whole grains over polished grains and bleached flour.

5. a. Jack Nelson, a reporter for the *Los Angeles Times,* began his career by exposing illegal gambling activities in Biloxi, Mississippi. He did his job so effectively that he himself was investigated by a Senate Crime Probe.
   b. In 1953 his story about political corruption in Hinesville, Georgia, resulted in grand jury indictments of forty-four townspeople.
   c. When Nelson covered the Hinesville trial, he was mobbed and nearly lynched by the townspeople, harassed by law officers, and later arrested on false charges.
   d. In 1959 Nelson wrote several articles exposing dangerous and unethical practices in Georgia Central State Hospital in Milledgeville. Nurses were being allowed to perform surgery, many doctors were taking drugs while on duty, and experimental drugs were being used on mental patients.
   e. More recently, Nelson wrote an article which indicated that at South Carolina State College, students alleged to have been conducting a gunfight with the police had in most cases been shot in the back or in the soles of their feet.

6. a. Guide dog puppies are farmed out to selected 4-H Club youngsters in whose homes the pups learn basic obedience, become accustomed to children, and are housebroken.

b. Potential guide dogs for the blind must learn early to ride in cars and to accept affection from other people.

c. For three to five months they are rigorously trained to avoid obstacles.

d. Before they are entrusted with guiding the blind, the dogs must learn to contend with ditches, falling objects, revolving doors, flights of stairs, and traffic.

_____

_____

_____

_____

7. a. In 1933, before Congress passed NRA legislation, workers in San Jose, California, were paid an hourly wage of as little as 17½ cents, which wouldn't even buy a pound of butter.

b. People worked from ten to fourteen hours a day, with an hour for lunch and a half-hour for supper.

c. Most jobs did not allow workers to go to the bathroom except during the lunch and supper break. There was no coffee break.

d. At the canneries, men hoping to find work stood in lines that were sometimes several blocks long.

e. If a worker couldn't keep up with the pace of the work or talked back to a boss, he was fired on the spot and replaced by one of the hungry men from the lines outside.

f. No unemployment insurance, no food stamps or food packages, and no welfare were available to the person after he was fired.

g. There were no unions.

_____

_____

_____

_____

8. a. In 1969 the Nevada Cement Company doubled the capacity of its plant at Fernley, near the Truckee River, by operating an old kiln without a satisfactory filter.

b. The air in nearby communities became so polluted with cement dust that early in 1970 a Nevada District Court judge stated that their operation was "a public nuisance" and in violation of Nevada state law. He ordered the company to have a secondary filtration system in operation within six months.

c. The company, however, didn't start work on the filtration system until three hours before it was supposed to go into operation.

d. Twelve months later, on May 1, 1971, the filtration system was finally completed.

e. During the eighteen months before the secondary filter was installed, an estimated 10.9 million pounds of cement waste was illegally discharged into the air over the communities of Fernley and Wadsworth.

f. For a while after May 1, the air was much better. Then the pollution began again. It became so bad that by autumn 1971 a group of eight-five citizens sued the company for damages.
g. On November 24, 1971, Judge Richard L. Waters of the local Nevada District Court found against the company. He ordered the company to pay the citizens bringing suit $540,000 in specific and general damages and $1.4 million in punitive damages.
h. Pollution continued, however, with cement dust spreading out for about a mile over the countryside. Spokesmen for the citizens' group have charged that the pollution increased after the court rendered its decision against the company.
i. The company plans to appeal the decision in the Nevada Supreme Court.

_____

_____

_____

9. a. "Hands" Bickerstaff, tight end for the Montpelier Mountebanks, has, of course, only two hands. But Hank Strangle, coach of the Gopher Prairie Cyclones, swears he has at least three. Hands caught eight passes, four for touchdowns, against the Cyclones last week.
b. Each of Hands's hands is eleven inches long and six inches wide.
c. In high school he had a nickname, which, although undoubtedly amusing to his friends, is unprintable.
d. Hands is especially outstanding on wet days. His coach, "Dusty" Miller, avows that "when it rains and everyone else is dropping the ball, that guy grows webs between his fingers."
e. In the national championship game, which the Mountebanks won 62 to 28, Hands caught six passes for touchdowns. The scorekeepers lost track of his other catches.
f. After the game Hands, with his customary modesty and brevity, said, "If I can touch 'em, I can catch 'em."

_____

_____

_____

10. a. During the Second World War, the United States, Russia, China, and India (then part of the British Empire) were allies against the Axis nations.
b. Five years later, in the Korean War, the United States (whose troops composed the largest part of the U.N. military forces) was fighting China in North Korea. Russia was sympathetic to North Korea and China and openly aided them with war material. India was sympathetic to the United States and South Korea.

c. Twelve years later, in Indochina, Russia and China, though quarreling neighbors, helped North Vietnam in its war against South Vietnam and the United States.

d. In 1971, China and the United States were diplomatically aligned in their support of Pakistan's opposition to India. Russia, however, supported India and opposed China and the United States.

_____

_____

_____

_____

EXERCISE 9: *Do exactly as you did in the preceding exercise.*

1. a. In September 1971 most of the inmates of the State Prison at Attica, New York, were blacks and Puerto Ricans.

   b. A spokesman for the black prisoners blamed the riot at Attica on the "most unmitigated oppression wrought by the racist administration network of this prison."

   c. The prisoners demanded freedom, total amnesty, and guaranteed transportation to a "non-imperialistic country" where they would receive political asylum.

   d. The prisoners also demanded that several people, including Huey Newton of the Black Panthers and representatives of the Black Muslims and the Puerto Rican Young Lords, be allowed to inspect the prison.

   e. Black Panther Chairman Bobby Seale went to Attica and spoke to the prisoners.

   f. Governor Rockefeller sent Herman Badillo, the first Puerto Rican to be elected to Congress, to Attica to speak to the prisoners.

_____

_____

_____

_____

2. a. Svetlana Stalin's brother Jacob died while being held captive by the Nazis in the Second World War.

   b. Her other brother, Vasily, died in 1962 under mysterious circumstances.

   c. When Svetlana Stalin was sixteen, she discovered that her mother's death had been a suicide rather than one by natural causes.

   d. Her husband, an Indian named Brajish Singh, was discriminated against in the Soviet Union and died there.

   e. Svetlana's father, Joseph Stalin, was discredited after his death and reviled in the Soviet Union.

3. a. Women shoplifters sometimes wear a garment called "booster bloomers," over-sized bloomers into which stolen articles can be dropped.
   b. A purse with a false bottom will hold jewelry and other small items.
   c. Small pilfered items can also be hidden in an umbrella.
   d. Some women shoplifters spirit out small pieces of jewelry in their shoes, their gloves, and even under their hats.

4. a. During the autumn of 1971, a five-man team of General Accounting Office investigators spent five weeks in Cambodia preparing a report on the effects of U.S. and South Vietnamese bombings there.
   b. They assert that since the spring of 1970, when American and South Vietnamese bombing of Cambodia began, more than 2 million Cambodians have been driven from their homes.
   c. They say that the bombing is a "very significant cause of civilian casualties."
   d. Tens of thousands of Cambodians have had to flee to neighboring Laos, Thailand, and South Vietnam.
   e. More than a half-million refugees have fled to Phnom Penh, the Cambodian capital, almost doubling the population of that already overcrowded city.
   f. We are not at war with Cambodia.

5. a. The paving of large land areas around Lake Tahoe prevents melting snow from being absorbed by the earth and causes it instead to flow into the lake, raising its normal level.
   b. Street sweepings and salt used to melt road ice flow into the lake, killing some kinds of marine life.
   c. Fertilizers from golf courses and the waste matter from countless septic tanks also end up in Lake Tahoe.

d. Denuded hillsides, cut up by construction bulldozers, drain their mud into the lake water.

_____

_____

_____

_____

6. a. In 1810 George Gordon, Lord Byron, swam the Hellespont, a treacherous strait that separates Europe from Asia.
   b. At the age of twenty-three, upon earning world literary fame for his first two published works, Lord Byron gave away all his royalties in order to maintain his image as "an aristocratic amateur."
   c. During the next few years, Byron was active—in the House of Lords as an extreme political liberal and friend of the dispossessed, and in society as a man who could not leave women alone.
   d. In 1816 a scandal involving Byron and his half-sister Augusta Leigh forced him to leave England permanently.
   e. In 1824 Byron organized and led a group of fighting men to assist the Greeks in their war against the Turks.
   f. Byron died of a fever in Missolonghi, Greece, just after his thirty-sixth birthday.

_____

_____

_____

_____

7. a. Stored blood, so crucial to lifesaving transfusions, can be kept only about three weeks before the red cells begin to disintegrate.
   b. The white cells in stored blood often cause a sensitization reaction, which may result in chills, fever, and, in rare cases, death.
   c. If stored blood harbors the hepatitis virus, the dangerous disease may be transmitted to transfusion patients.
   d. Donors of rare blood types sometimes cannot be found in time to help patients who have lost blood in accidents.
   e. Person-to-person transfusions are not often practicable.

_____

_____

_____

_____

8. a. On December 15, 1971, at a meeting of the United Nations Security Council, Pakistan's foreign minister Zulfikar Ali Bhutto rose and said to Russia's Jacob Malik, "You pump up your chest and you pound the table. You don't talk like Comrade Malik but like Czar Malik. . . . I am glad you are smiling. I am not. . . . My heart is in tears."

   b. "Mr. President," he continued, "we have seen filibustering over whether the Council would be ready to meet at 9:30 or whether bed and breakfast required that it meet at 11:00; [in the meantime] millions are dying."

   c. Bhutto continued, "Let's build a monument for the veto. Let's build a monument for impotence and incapacity."

   d. Then, just before rising and leaving the chamber, he said, "Mr. President, I am not a rat. I have never ratted in my life. I have faced assassination attempts. I've faced imprisonment. . . . Today I am not ratting, but I am leaving your Security Council."

   e. Outside the chambers, he said, "I hate this body. I don't want to see their faces again. I would rather go back to a destroyed Pakistan."

---

9. a. Rico Carty, who comes from the Dominican Republic and is an outfielder for the Atlanta Braves, wears a perpetual smile.

   b. Carty always catches the ball with one hand, and tosses it to the fans.

   c. Carty once slugged teammate Hank Aaron.

   d. Carty describes himself as "crazy hitter until two strikes, then I look for strike zone."

   e. At the plate, Carty cocks his bat straight up in the air like an exclamation point.

---

10. a. Coke Infante, sometimes called "the Mayor" of San Francisco's North Beach, is over 6 feet tall and weighs over 200 pounds.

   b. Coke wears a sleeveless snakeskin coat, a bright yellow hat, and basketball shoes.

   c. He sports a huge Garibaldi-style mustache.

   d. Coke likes to roll "liar's dice" for high stakes in his own Broadway topless bar.

   e. He is well read and can converse intelligently and knowledgeably, especially with beautiful women, most of whom seem charmed with Coke.

   f. In twenty-five years, though Coke has had to defend himself countless times, no one has ever seen him lose a fight in the Broadway bar.

_____

_____

_____

_____

11. a. In Rome in November 1971, Dr. Norman Borlaug of Iowa, "father of the 'green revolution'" and a 1970 Nobel Prize winner, attacked what he called the "irresponsible environmentalists" who are trying to ban DDT and certain other pesticides and fertilizers.
   b. He called his opponents "hysterical lobbyists."
   c. He says that if these environmentalists get their way, the danger of world starvation will be much greater than the danger of death from chemical poisoning.
   d. Noting that "50 percent of the present world population is undernourished and 65 percent malnourished," he said that this situation would worsen if the "current crusades of the privileged environmentalists in the United States" are successful.
   e. He blamed Rachel Carson's novel *Silent Spring* for starting the movement against DDT.
   f. He said that if pesticides were "completely banned" in the United States, there would be "50 percent crop losses" and food prices would go up 400-500 percent.

_____

_____

_____

_____

12. a. The consensus of scientists throughout the world is that pesticides such as DDT, which do not break down chemically, are poisoning the soil, the waters of the world, and all animal life (including man) at an accelerating rate.
   b. In the opinion of these scientists, the defenders of pesticides ignore the fact that insects are developing immunities to the poisons while humans and other large animals are not.
   c. They also argue that the use of pesticides is only one of the many ways in which we are polluting the environment.
   d. This pollution, they argue, is so vast and is accelerating at such a frightening rate that their warnings, far from being hysterical, are probably understatements.
   e. Their major worry, however, is that very few people are listening to them.

_____

_____

_____

_____

13. a. In a typical supper-club performance, comedian Marty Melon is likely to yell, "Dig the nose on the guy coming in. He could hire out as a bloodhound."

b. When a lady accidentally spilled her cocktail during one of his performances, Melon asked, "Been drinking long, honey?"

c. Melon always tells his audiences, "You think you're rating *me*. But I've been rating you, and I just laid the lowest score this month on you."

d. He once quipped to an entering celebrity with a reputation for wife-stealing, "Hey, Bennie, go home. All the girls here are single."

_____

_____

_____

_____

EXERCISE 10: *Choose one of the following topic sentences and then write a 100-200 word paragraph supporting it as factually as you can. Do not rely solely on memory for the facts. Consult outside sources such as books, magazines, and newspapers for information, or else use actual observations.*

1. Other things being equal, a solid sphere will roll down an inclined plane faster than a solid object of any other shape.
2. Team sports teach players to subordinate their individual goals to those of the team.
3. Most sports, whether team or individual, teach the competitor that winning is the only thing that really counts.
4. I agree with the old Persian saying "The face of the winner is like a rose; the face of the loser is like a graveyard."
5. There is much truth in the Turkish proverb that says, "He who would speak the truth should have one foot in the stirrup."
6. It is within each person's power to perform a few acts aimed at preserving the cleanliness or beauty of the environment.
7. Cats are very independent pets.
8. The youth of America show great variety in their dress.
9. During the last few years American college students have expressed their disapproval of standard college curricula in several constructive ways.
10. One of the reasons for the popularity of the song "Desiderata" is that its life-affirming words do not offend any ethnic, social, or philosophical group.
11. Chewing gum allows us to do something physical on the many occasions when we are supposed to appear completely inactive.
12. The freedom to dress and groom ourselves as we please enables us to express some of our tastes and values in very explicit ways.
13. For many people, writing is a disagreeable task because it is such a solitary activity.

14. For most people, writing is a disagreeable task because it reveals many personal weaknesses.
15. Writing gives us a unique opportunity to express ourselves.
16. A fire in a fireplace tends to distract us from whatever we might be trying to do.
17. My twelve-year-old sister has more freedom than I had at her age.
18. To be spoiled is to have unreasonable expectations.
19. Getting up in the morning is a loathsome necessity.
20. Getting up in the morning is one of the most stimulating events of the day.
21. Our dog is a nuisance to our neighbors.
22. One of George C. Scott's strengths as an actor is his versatility.
23. Our opinionated next-door neighbor reminds us of Archie Bunker because of his beliefs.
24. Baby-sitting is a comfortable way to earn money.
25. The TV show "Sanford and Son" illustrates differences in the values of two generations.
26. There are many widely different subgroups among the people generally known as "hippies."
27. The names of many of today's rock groups show originality and imagination.

2
Unity

Unity is a word encountered in most books on writing. Defined most simply, unity might be called "the quality of oneness," a union of related parts that form a harmonious whole. As such, unity is found in virtually every area of civilized life, from philosophy to music to architecture, sports, engineering, politics, and even cooking. Good writing, too, requires unity of structure, whether that writing takes the form of a novel, an essay, or even a single paragraph.

What is unity in writing and how does it work in a paragraph? Often, an effective way to define an object or quality is to begin by showing what it is *not*. The following student paragraph could serve as a case in point:

(1) To me the most outstanding feature of Cerebros College is the athletic department. (2) This feature makes Cerebros different from the college that I attended in the past. (3) The athletics there were in sorry shape. (4) But here at Cerebros the athletic performances are really exciting. (5) I don't think a college would amount to much if it didn't have an intramural athletic program. (6) These after-school activities help in many ways. (7) They help raise funds for other school activities and give the student something to do besides just studying. (8) I definitely think that the student should study, granted, but he must also have fun at social events and dances. (9) I met the girl I go with at a school dance. (10) In conclusion, the student shouldn't come to school just to be there, but so that he or she can participate in its functions.

Whatever we might say about this paragraph, we could not call it organized or unified. Let's examine it in detail.

In his topic sentence, the writer promises us that he will discuss the outstanding qualities of the physical education department of the college. But before long he wanders from his prescribed subject. In sentence 2, he informs us that he's had experience at a different college, but that bit of information hardly proves that Cerebros has a good athletic department. Sentences 4 and 5 present the writer's opinion but provide no factual evidence that would help fulfill his "promise." By sentence 6 the writer has forgotten that he's "plugging" the physical education department, and he begins to lecture on the benefits of extracurricular activities for the student. Sentence 9 discusses the writer's social life and apparently has little to do with the physical education department at Cerebros. Since the writer fails to include even one convincing *fact* in support of the topic sentence, it soon becomes obvious to the impatient reader that he has been taken on a tour by a rambling mind.

Let's review the unrelated areas covered in this student's paragraph:

1. The writer's experience at an out-of-state college.
2. The inadequacy of the athletic program at his former school.
3. The benefits to be derived from after-school activities.
4. Recommendations on how the student can avoid excessive study.
5. How the writer found romance at Cerebros.

Obviously, if the ideal paragraph should develop in detail only one of the areas mentioned above, this paragraph is far from ideal. Like many beginning writers, this student has fallen asleep at the wheel. His tour has resulted in something resembling an accident; that's the kindest thing one can say about the paragraph.

But fortunately the student revised his opening paragraph. Later in the semester he was able to produce the following:

(1) Each week of the semester, the physical education department at Cerebros provides the student with many opportunities to enjoy healthful recreation. (2) On Monday and Wednesday evenings there is recreational dancing from seven until ten under the direction of Mrs. Bell, who sometimes teaches the students Balkan dances. (3) Tuesdays at eight Mr. Gardner conducts physical exercise classes for the men while Miss Tillotson teaches the women how to keep fit. (4) Men's and women's classes both include instruction in a number of Oriental defensive disciplines such as judo, karate, shing-yee, tai-chi, and pa-qua. (5) Tuesdays also feature intramural basketball in the main gym during the winter months and badminton and tennis on the outdoor courts in the spring, when the evenings are longer. (6) The physical education department also welcomes students to the "Friday Flicks," shown free in the main gym throughout the school year. (7) As can be seen, there is a weekly recreational event to suit nearly every preference.

Several characteristics of this revision make it more effective than the original paragraph. For one thing, the writer has made the main part of each sentence (see underlining) relate to the controlling idea of the paragraph, "healthful recreation." By doing so, he has avoided skipping around to unrelated subjects that distract the reader's attention from the major issue of the paragraph.

34

As a rule, unity is achieved by relating the *main clause* of each supporting sentence directly to the controlling idea of the topic sentence. Allow no sentence in the paragraph to deviate from that pattern. If you have an intriguing sentence or an idea that does not relate directly to the controlling idea, suppress the urge to write it down, at least temporarily. Perhaps it can be still used. Later in this chapter you will find out how to use material that is somewhat related to the subject but not strictly unified with the controlling idea of the paragraph.

Main Clause Unity

At this point we will quickly review the difference between a main (independent) clause and a subordinate (dependent) one, since unity depends, for the most part, on main clauses being related to the topic sentence. You probably remember that a *clause* is a group of words that contains a subject and a verb (underlined in the following examples, with one line beneath the subject and two beneath the verb):

1. After Grabowski played lacrosse at Wisconsin in the thirties
2. Tarzan could spare some time from fighting evil.
3. Whenever Sam Suggins got liquored up
4. He ought to take a course in public speaking.
5. After the junior prom became a campus joke

The above constructions are clauses, but they are not all main (independent) clauses. Examples 2 and 4 are independent, for they can stand by themselves. But examples 1, 3, and 5 are dependent (subordinate) clauses; the beginning word in each—a subordinator—warns the reader that he is dealing with a construction that cannot stand by itself. Take a perfectly good sentence:

Tarzan could spare some time from fighting evil.

Obviously, such a group of words is perfectly capable of standing alone. But place a subordinator in front of it and see what happens:

If Tarzan could spare some time from fighting evil,

What was an independent construction now needs help from something else. Without help, the clause remains a fragment, a construction you've probably heard discussed before.

To return for a moment to the Ape Man, let's suppose the topic of your paragraph was Tarzan's social shortcomings and how they could be overcome. You might aid the subordinate clause in the following manner:

If Tarzan could spare some time from fighting evil, he'd do well to take a course in public speaking.

35

or, to reverse the order,

> Tarzan ought to take a course in public speaking *whenever* he can spare some time from fighting evil.

Notice that it makes no difference where the subordinate clause is placed. It can begin or end the sentence. The important point is that the *main* (independent) part of the sentence is the part that proves or supports the controlling idea, and in the above example the controlling idea expresses Tarzan's need for social sophistication. We are not directly concerned, therefore, with his fight against evil, although it makes an interesting *lesser* detail. You needn't throw it away. But you must place it out of the way of the real business of the paragraph as promised in the controlling idea. In short, subordinate Tarzan's fight against evil to his need for social improvement and you'll keep your paragraph unified, with all the main ideas supporting the controlling idea.

For a better idea of what can happen when a writer gets careless with clauses, let's look at a paragraph that was criticized by an instructor for lacking unity. Subjects and verbs of main clauses are underlined:

> (1) According to an essay in the June 5, 1972, issue of *Time,* many of Italy's cultural landmarks and art treasures are being abused, disfigured, or destroyed. (2) In allowing drivers to use the ancient piazza of a cathedral in Lodi as a parking lot, Italian authorities revealed their evident conviction that the area couldn't support itself as a landmark. (3) Officials in Ferrara appeared equally indifferent when they allowed mechanics to use a medieval basilica as a garage, complete with hydraulic lifts and an area for washing cars. (4) In Salerno one night, truckers employed by land developers drove up and attached chains from their vehicles to a little thirteenth-century church, pulling the entire structure down to make room for a modern building. (5) Public agencies squabble over their cut of a $400 million emergency restoration fund for Venice while a painting by Bellini is stolen from an unguarded church. (6) The danger to these treasures seems immediate; a European travel poster summed up the situation: "Visit Italy Now, Before the Italians Destroy It."

Not a bad paragraph, you are probably thinking. And you have a point. The paragraph is a bit underdeveloped, but it's literate and clearly phrased. Yet, if we all agree that the controlling idea is the promise the writer makes to the reader, we have to admit that in this paragraph that promise has not been kept. For the controlling idea—*abused, disfigured, or destroyed*—is not directly supported in the paragraph. True, certain facts are provided that relate to the controlling idea, but instead of appearing in the main clause of each sentence, these pertinent facts turn up, like poor cousins, in dependent constructions. The main clauses (underlined in the paragraph) seem to support some other idea. You might, for instance, try checking each clause underlined in the above paragraph against either of the following topic sentences:

> Priceless Italian landmarks and art works are being jeopardized by official indifference.
> Italy's legacy to the world is endangered by bureaucracy.

But, alas, these are not the ideas that the writer promised to develop.

Again, let's remember that support for the topic sentence should be provided in the main (independent) clauses in the paragraph. So if a writer decides that a new set of facts is more exciting than his original set, he must change his topic sentence to control the new facts. Had the above student, for instance, really wished to write primarily about bureaucratic indifference to the fate of Italy's art works, he should have constructed his topic sentence with that in mind and then used facts that would have illustrated the *causes* rather than the *effects* of the officials' attitude toward Italy's art treasures. Compare the student's original paragraph with a revised version. Subjects and verbs of main clauses have been underlined:

> (1) According to an essay in the June 5, 1972, issue of *Time,* many of Ital's cultural landmarks and art treasures are being abused, disfigured, or destroyed. (2) In Lodi, townspeople made a parking lot out of an ancient piazza while authorities evidently condoned the eyesore by failing to prohibit such activity. (3) Displaying equal indifference, Ferrara officials permitted mechanics to transform a medieval church into a garage where cars are washed and lubricated. (4) In Salerno, truckers demolished a little thirteenth-century church one night by attaching chains to it and pulling down the walls with their vehicles. (5) In Venice, a Bellini painting was stolen from an unguarded church while public agencies squabbled about their cut of a $400 million emergency restoration fund. (6) The danger to these treasures seems immediate; a European travel poster summed up the situation: "Visit Italy Now, Before the Italians Destroy It."

You might argue that the revised version is not drastically different from its original. And again you'd have a point. Actually, many of the same facts and statistics have been used to support the topic sentence in the rewrite. The difference is that in the revision, the important facts and statistics have been repositioned in the main clauses, instead of being placed in the dependent parts of sentences.

To test main clause unity, the student might try underlining the subject and verb in the main clause of each of his own sentences, using one line under the subject and two under the verb or predicate. If the independent clause of each sentence relates directly to the controlling idea, the writer has probably achieved a reasonable degree of unity. Do you remember that "quality of oneness," that "harmonious whole" we made such an issue over at the beginning of this chapter? Well, the above paragraph begins to move toward that ideal.

Gaining Unity Through Subordination

We have been discussing the concept of *subordination* with regard to the above examples. Subordination might be defined most simply as the placing of certain ideas in less important positions than other ideas in the sentence. A subordinate clause or phrase, like a subordinate rank in military service, is a part that depends on another, more responsible, part for support or direction. A subordinate construction usually has less weight or significance than the part that it helps qualify or modify. Consider the following sentences:

1. Sergeant Hawkins crossed the bamboo thicket.
2. He darted to the top of a small incline.
3. At the top he was struck in the foot by a sniper's bullet.

If one were writing about the above incident, which sentence would he want to emphasize as the most significant or important? Most people, of course, would choose sentence 3; it's the climax of this set of events, and it describes the injury—perhaps serious—of a soldier. Therefore, sentences 1 and 2 are of less weight and import here. If the writer were faced with the task of fitting all three of these short sentences into a single more sophisticated sentence, then, how could he arrange them? One possibility might be the following:

> After Sergeant Hawkins crossed a bamboo thicket and darted to the top of a small incline, he was struck in the foot by a sniper's bullet.

What has the writer done in this instance with sentences 1 and 2? How have they been positioned in relation to sentence 3? They may be said to have been *subordinated* (placed in a position of less importance) to sentence 3. Sentences 1 and 2 have been blended into a single clause that the writer has made dependent by placing it after a subordinator (*After*). By subordinating these two short clauses to the more important one, the writer has positioned all these individual ideas in proper relation to one another.

To the student, subordination may not seem, at first glance, to have much to do with unity. Yet, if the writer of the following paragraph had known as much as you now know about subordination, he probably wouldn't have been penalized for lack of unity:

> (1) As the world's food requirements increase along with the growing population, theorists are discussing means of controlling and domesticating sea creatures. (2) The theories advanced in Arthur C. Clarke's book *The Deep Range* sound like science fiction. (3) Clarke suggests that whales be kept in herds through the use of ultrasonic fences stationed along their migration routes. (4) Clarke's alternative is even more bizarre. (5) He recommends that killer whales be captured. (6) They could be trained to herd and guard the larger whales. (7) And then there are oysters. (8) Experiments are being conducted in which oysters are raised on columns of empty shells that are attached to wires and suspended from underwater platforms. (9) This keeps the oysters safe from predators that feed on the bottom. (10) Underwater ranches are places to be set aside for marine husbandry. (11) At these places, turtles and other wandering but nonmigratory creatures could be fattened for the food market. (12) If even one of the ideas cited above proves feasible, it could supply some of the food needs of a swelling world population.

Not much analysis is needed to see rather quickly that the controlling idea (*means of controlling and domesticating*) is not supported in every sentence that follows it. Sentences 3, 5, 6, 8, 9, and 11 all seem to support the promise, since each of these deals with a situation in which marine life could be domesticated and raised as an eventual source of food for humans. But what about sentences 2, 4, 7, and 10? Should the writer take the easy way out and get rid of these unrelated sentences? In this instance, the writer refused to be defeated. He remembered that it was permissible to incorporate in a paragraph material that was not directly related to the topic sentence. He simply subordinated the sentences that didn't deal directly with controlling and domesticating sea creatures to those that did. The result is the following revision:

(1) As the world's food requirements increase along with the growing population, theorists are discussing means of controlling and domesticating sea creatures. (2) In a theory that sounds like science fiction, Arthur C. Clarke, in his book *The Deep Range*, recommends that whales be herded through the use of ultrasonic fences stationed along their migratory routes. (3) As a bizarre alternative, Clarke suggests that killer whales be captured and trained to herd and guard the larger whales. (4) Although the technique is still only in the experimental stage, oysters have been raised on columns of empty shells suspended on wires from underwater platforms to keep them safe from bottom-dwelling predators. (5) On undersea "ranches," turtles and other wandering, nonmigratory marine creatures could be fattened for the food market. (6) If even one of the theories described above proves feasible, it could help fill some of the world's food requirements.

Note the ways in which the revision improves on the original:

1. Most important, it focuses all the independent clauses on the controlling idea, making the paragraph unified. (You might try running a check of your own by underlining the subjects and verbs in the main clauses.)
2. It cuts down the number of sentences from twelve to six.
3. It avoids the repetition found in the original paragraph.
4. It smooths the flow of the prose, making the writing less choppy by using certain transitional phrases. (Transitional phrases will be discussed in a later chapter.)

You'll probably admit that subordination was worth trying in the above writer's case. The returns in better prose were worth the investment of time. What resulted was writing that was more "muscular," since the writer compressed his paragraph through subordination. Subordination, then, helps achieve unity, to be sure. In addition, it can help the student to cut the fat out of his writing, to work his prose into solid bone and muscle. And who wouldn't enjoy being stronger in one way or another?

Summary: Unity

1. Unity occurs in a paragraph in which all the sentences of the paragraph relate to the controlling idea and fulfill its "promise."
2. Strict unity is best achieved by relating the main clause of each supporting sentence to the controlling idea of the topic sentence.
3. If the writer wishes to use in his paragraph ideas that are not directly related to the main idea, he should position these ideas in subordinate clauses or phrases. Then they may be included in the paragraph.
4. To test main clause unity, the student should underline the subject and verb of each main clause and check these against the controlling idea of the paragraph.

EXERCISE 11: *All but one of the sentences in each of the following groups have a common subject and would constitute a unified paragraph. Pick the sentence that* does *not* belong *and place the letter of that sentence in the first blank. In the second blank, summarize the topic that unifies the remaining sentences.*

1. a. In several eastern European countries last year, cold early rains drowned much of the seed in the farmers' fields.
   b. Hailstorms along the Danube Valley flattened young plants.
   c. Floods in Poland took their toll of new crops, which were washed away in the waters.
   d. A lack of modern machinery compounded last year's difficulties in many eastern European countries.
   e. Locusts ate vast portions of the wheat crop in the Ukraine.

_____ _____

2. a. In one of his last bouts, Sugar Ray Robinson missed repeatedly with his jab in early rounds against Joey Archer.
   b. By the third round Archer was hitting Robinson almost at will with jabs and crosses.
   c. Archer used a combination jab and cross in the middle rounds to harass the veteran fighter.
   d. Sugar Ray began his boxing career when Archer was two years old.
   e. Archer found the range with a hook once or twice in the late rounds, but failed to down Robinson.

_____ _____

3. a. Western singer Doyle "Windy" Meadows owns a company that controls apartment buildings in Los Angeles, condominiums in Hawaii, and ranch land in Montana.
   b. Meadows himself owns a nine-acre ranch in Las Vegas, Nevada.
   c. Conservation-minded, Meadows has influenced legislation to control and punish the slaughter of predatory birds—particularly eagles—in Montana and Nevada.
   d. He has two Bentley automobiles, a Rolls-Royce, and an XKE.
   e. He flies to conferences in his own Lear jet.
   f. Recently he has taken up the breeding and raising of Arabian thoroughbred horses as a hobby.

_____ _____

4. a. In most East Coast metropolitan areas, an 8:00 P.M. dinner invitation often really means that the host wants his guests to arrive at 8:30.
   b. In Catskill summer resorts, a "sevenish" party seldom commences before 8:00 or 8:30, and "on time" is any time before midnight.
   c. In fixing a time for a get-together, hosts in the Midwest usually mean more or less what they say on the invitation.

d. Guests in Los Angeles tend to be the least time-conscious of all, sometimes remaining at parties until five or six o'clock in the morning.

e. In Germany, a considerate guest will arrive at the time indicated by the host.

---

5. a. Woodrow Wilson's Ph.D. thesis, "Congressional Government," was an original study of comparative political institutions.

b. In 1887 Wilson's article "The Study of Administration" generated student interest in a sophisticated government.

c. "Constitutional Government in the United States," a treatise compiled from Wilson's lectures at Princeton, is still studied with interest in the United States.

d. Sigmund Freud and William C. Bullitt, however, dismiss much of Wilson's writing as "beautiful but empty rhetoric."

e. Wilson's book *The State* is still used in many classrooms.

---

6. a. On the late-night TV show "Monster Movies," host Bela Profuso is apt to introduce a film like *Attack of the Crab Monsters* by saying, "This flick isn't to be confused with the U.S. Army training film of the same name."

b. Profuso called a film entitled *Women of the Prehistoric Planet* "a training film for the Women's Liberation Front."

c. Profuso said that a film called *Creeping Unknown* was about "a vampire with acne."

d. Profuso has remarked, "My show may not be a heavyweight, but it probably won't corrupt anyone."

e. He recently opened a show by saying, "We've had a lot of cards and letters concerning tonight's movie, but we're going to show it to you anyway."

---

7. a. In his first year as a professional football player, Los Angeles Rams' Bruno Prewicz gained 237 yards from scrimmage in a game against the Chicago Bears.

b. He scored 21 touchdowns to establish a new NFL record.

c. Prewicz was a three-time All-American from Penn State.

d. In a game against the Steelers in the Los Angeles Coliseum, Prewicz scored on sprints of 67, 82, 83, and 91 yards respectively.

e. In a game against the St. Louis Cardinals, Prewicz caught a 20-yard pass and outran the whole defense to score the winning touchdown.

---

8. a. Some men seek adventure like that found in big-game hunting because of a competitive instinct, a need to assert themselves.

b. Some are loners who prefer more solitary activities, like lion-taming.

c. Others satisfy their egos by challenging "killer" mountains.

d. Still others find that cave-exploring or scuba-diving adds meaning and zest to life.

e. Most adventurers will readily agree, however, that no undertaking is quite so hazardous as marriage.

---

9. a. When Sir Francis Chichester, the famed British yacht skipper, was seventy-five days out of England, his automatic steering device was smashed by giant waves.

b. A day out of Sydney, Australia, Chichester's craft was almost flipped over on its side by seventy-five-knot winds.

c. Chichester had set a record by sailing farther than any lone mariner ever had without sighting land.

d. After he rounded Cape Horn and headed home to England, Chichester found he was running low on supplies; he also developed an abscess in his elbow and had to take a painkiller.

---

10. a. Rising actress Joanie Malibu, who lives in an abandoned aviary on an old Beverly Hills estate, visited Hanoi to show her sympathy with the victims of American bombing.

b. She once conducted a sleep-in to show support for the Indians on Alcatraz Island.

c. Joanie sings first contralto in the choir at Holy Mother Episcopal Church in nearby Santa Rosana.

d. She recently told reporters that she had had a brief affair with Fidel Castro.

e. Last month Joanie published an article that called for the nomination of a woman vice-president, the institution of universal legal abortion, and the impeachment of the Chief Justice of the Supreme Court.

EXERCISE 12: *Do exactly as you did in the preceding exercise.*

1. a. E. Harvey Pummel's contributions to charity amount to about $20,000 annually.

b. Pummel is the secretary of Friends of the Opera in his city, and through his time and monetary contributions, he has helped make the symphony orchestra a successful venture.

c. He is a generous friend to his church and has even preached occasionally as a lay minister.

d. Pummel, who is president of a large manufacturing company, neither smokes nor drinks, and he strongly disapproves of gambling.

e. He personally lent his name and office to a campaign last year to collect money for disabled children.

---

2. a. Statistics reveal that annual worldwide food production increases by 1 to 1.5 percent, while population increases by 2 percent.
   b. In California, prime agricultural land is being paved over at the rate of 375 acres per day.
   c. "Already, automobiles occupy more space in America than people do," reports Edward Crafts of the U.S. Bureau of Outdoor Recreation.
   d. It has been estimated that in order to stay above the starvation level, we will have to double the world's food production in the next three decades.
   e. We will need to quadruple it within the next half-century.

3. a. In the small southern California town of Glendorne, J. Harriman McDonald owns a foundry, two drugstores, a newspaper, a small packing house, and 10,000 acres of prime citrus and avocado orchards—all of which have employed minority group members and the handicapped for the past twenty-five years.
   b. McDonald, who likes to pass his time in the smoky foundry, is fond of saying, "Give a man a chance to earn an honest living, and he'll surprise both you and himself with how well he'll do."
   c. McDonald heads the board of trustees of the local junior college, and he is chairman of the city council, which votes on all important measures affecting the community.
   d. McDonald got his start during the Depression, when, as a young drifter, he was hired to cut some firewood for a local rancher and stayed to marry the rancher's daughter and supervise his father-in-law's orchards.
   e. McDonald personally contributed a quarter-million dollars to charity last year, and he annually sponsors several students from minority groups as well as foreign exchange students at the college.

4. a. "The human knee was never meant for a game like football," said an NFL quarterback after tearing several knee ligaments in a Sunday game.
   b. A linebacker in the AFL has had seven operations on both knees over a six-year period, yet he continues to play.
   c. The knee is held together mainly by ligaments and cartilage and is not well adapted to the kind of sideways contact it frequently receives on the pro gridiron.
   d. Joe Namath needed major knee surgery before he ever played a full season in the pros.
   e. Unlike the knee, the shoulder and the hip are fastened by powerful ball-and-socket joints that can be twisted or flexed in several directions without undue strain.

5. a. Some critics believe that making marriage more difficult to enter into by instituting a thirty-day waiting period before the issuance of a license would influence couples to take marriage more seriously.

43

b. Sociologist Mervyn Cadwallader believes in establishing a flexible marriage contract that could be renewed every year if both parties are satisfied.

c. Statistics show that 715,000 divorces were granted in the United States in 1970, as compared with 485,000 in 1945.

d. A famous sociologist believes in a marital contract that would allow partners to decide at the outset not to have children.

e. Several well-known sociologists believe that a couple who marry with the intention of having a family should sign an agreement to this effect beforehand.

---

6. a. Among some undersea treasures recovered several years ago in the Bahamas is a silver crucifix two inches long.

b. Recovering treasure at such depths involves great risks to scuba divers.

c. Porcelain cups in perfect condition were found on a shipwreck off Puerto Rico.

d. A long chain of polished gold links was found in the Philippines.

e. Several thousand dollars worth of Spanish coins were taken from a wreck near Moss Landing, off the California coast.

---

7. a. In parts of California, many scenic stands of thousand-year-old sequoia redwoods are in danger of being harvested by lumber companies.

b. These trees have relatively shallow roots that like the slopes of deep canyons, where the trees find shelter from the winds.

c. Redwoods require heavy irrigation by rains from November through April.

d. To reach maturity, these giant sequoias need fog, which they absorb as moisture.

e. The sequoia redwoods prefer the black alluvial soil found in parts of northern California and southern Oregon.

---

8. a. The late West German Chancellor Konrad Adenauer was responsible for bringing Germany into the Atlantic Alliance.

b. Adenauer, who fully acknowledged Germany's guilt in the genocide of 6 million European Jews, arranged for $7 billion worth of reparations for survivors and their families.

c. Adenauer negotiated a treaty of friendship between old enemies, France and Germany.

d. In ten years of shrewd political leadership, he turned his nation into the third largest industrial state in the world.

e. Even as mayor of Cologne in the early 1930's, Adenauer was openly against Nazism.

---

9. a. Ernest Schoefer, a retired nursery owner, has planted beds of dahlias, snapdragons, and rhododendrons in a forty-nine-acre section of the Mendocino coastline that was a peat bog and rain forest when he bought it.

b. Through this forest, Schoefer has built two miles of paths that cross foot-bridges over trout streams.

c. Schoefer and his two assistants had to burn a vast amount of undergrowth to turn the acreage into a public garden.

d. Working with hand tools, they chopped away stumps, dug flower beds, and planted hundreds of ferns.

e. Schoefer's hard work has drawn the attention of Californians and Oregonians and added to Mendocino's drawing power as a tourist center.

---

10. a. Republican Mayor George Potluck of Quaker Heights believes strongly in catering to the business community and favors the interests of capital above those of labor.

b. Mayor Potluck approves heartily of U.S. participation in the war in Vietnam.

c. Potluck, a member of the board of trustees at the local college, is opposed to much emphasis on courses such as literature, art, and philosophy. "Give them meat and potato courses," he says.

d. The mayor is a lover of symphonic music and is so knowledgeable about it that he lectures on Beethoven and Mozart.

e. He backed Arizona Senator Barry Goldwater in the 1964 presidential race, vigorously campaigned for California Governor Ronald Reagan in 1966, and supported Richard Nixon in the 1968 and 1972 presidential elections.

f. The mayor personally led a movement to drive all "bohemian elements" out of Quaker Heights.

EXERCISE 13: *Do exactly as you did in the preceding exercises.*

1. a. When ace automobile racer Archie Magwirth finished a race at Detroit, Michigan, last year, he had huge blisters on his hands from gripping the wheel so savagely.

b. Magwirth, who is from Leeds, England, broke his left leg in a pile-up at the fairgrounds in Reading, Pennsylvania.

c. Three months later at Dayton, Ohio, he was badly burned when the cockpit wiring of his midget auto caught fire.

d. In April of last year, when Magwirth was the leading money winner, he flipped his car at a race in Fort Worth, Texas, and suffered a broken right arm.

e. He would have finished the season driving one-handed, but an appendicitis attack in Waukegan, Illinois, required immediate surgery and prevented him from finishing at all.

---

2. a. Major Marcus A. Reno, the scapegoat for the disastrous defeat at Little Big Horn, once broke a pool cue over the head of another officer during a hard-drinking evening.

b. Reno was court-martialed for looking through a parlor window one night at his commanding officer's daughter, whom he admired very much.

c. On the day of George Custer's defeat and death at Little Big Horn in 1876, Major Reno led his forces successfully against a Sioux party about four miles away and did not come to Custer's aid.

d. In 1879 Reno was accused of paying court to the wife of another officer.

e. On another occasion, an enraged Reno broke a chair through the window of a billiard room.

---

3. a. In 1966 the U.S. Embassy and American military leaders in Saigon commissioned a group of Americans with long experience in Vietnam to investigate the "pacification" program there.

b. They found, contrary to the Rand Corporation's conclusions (based on its 1965 investigations), that our bombing and shelling of areas in South Vietnam where Viet Cong were thought to be hiding was driving hundreds of thousands of refugees into city slums and concentration camps.

c. They went on to say that this was making Vietnamese peasants far more angry with us than with the Viet Cong, again contrary to the Rand Corporation's findings.

d. They recommended that this aspect of the pacification program be examined more closely, with the clear implication that the bombing of villages and fields should cease.

e. The recommendation was vetoed by our leaders, and the bombing and shelling continued.

---

4. a. Eastwood Bleachwell lifts weights every day and tries to surpass his own record, which he has posted in his garage.

b. He makes an annual trek into the wilds of Baffin Island to hunt the great brown bear.

c. Bleachwell, the thirty-eight-year-old president of a large manufacturing firm, also enjoys water-skiing and body-surfing.

d. Bleachwell's love of the rugged sporting life is shared by his beautiful wife, Yvonne.

e. He enjoys a heated game of tennis during his lunch hour each day.

---

5. a. In a recent game against the Vikings, Detroit's Melrose Lampwick ran the opening kickoff back for a touchdown.

b. In the second quarter Lampwick was tackled so hard by Dieter Schmidt, the Vikings' great linebacker, that he fumbled; but he recovered his own fumble.

c. Just before the half, Lampwick caught a touchdown pass from Sandor Szabel to move Detroit ahead.

d. On a quick opener, Lampwick ran 50 yards for a third-quarter score.

e. Five minutes later he won the game for Detroit by kicking a 45-yard field goal against a stiff wind.

6. a. Sports analyst and commentator H. Emmett "Sam" Breedlaw once asked former heavyweight champion Joe Louis, "Did you throw the first fight with Max Schmeling?"

b. When Pro Football Commissioner Roy Piper announced the merger of the National Football League and the American Football League, Breedlaw asked him, "Didn't the AFL force this merger by secretly making offers to NFL stars?"

c. When Piper replied that it wasn't true, Breedlaw shouted, "You know damned well it's true!"

d. Breedlaw once said of President Nixon, "I don't think Richard Nixon, while well motivated, is in touch with the reality of the contemporary American society." He added that Nixon was a better sports fan than he was a president.

e. When he returned from a recent trip to Italy, Breedlaw, a practicing Catholic, brought back a holy medal blessed by the Pope to his friend Muhammad Ali.

f. Breedlaw was recently told by friends that he gave the impression he knew more about a subject than anyone else. He replied, "What's so strange about that? As a matter of fact, I do."

7. a. A nationwide survey indicates that horror films featuring ghouls and monsters continue to lead Westerns (the next most popular type of film) by a 15 percent margin.

b. The first of the truly great "horror" stars was Lon Chaney, whose roles in *The Hunchback of Notre Dame* and *The Phantom of the Opera* made him world-famous.

c. Hungarian Bela Lugosi played Count Dracula with such evil charm that at one time in the mid-1930's he was receiving as much fan mail as Rudolph Valentino had a decade before.

d. American adults and children alike thrilled to Boris Karloff's great portrayal of Mary Shelley's Frankenstein monster.

8. a. Whitey Schultze, who has never strayed far outside the city limits of Kenosha, Wisconsin, always tells everybody at the "Sit 'n' Sip" that he fought in the Battle of the Bulge.

b. Whitey once informed the local scout troop that he had been a consultant to President Truman in Washington during the 1948 campaign.

c. Schultze claims credit for having helped rescue three mine workers at a cave-in south of Johnstown, Pennsylvania, in March 1939.

d. He insists that he turned down a gangster role in Hollywood during the 1930's in deference to George Raft, who eventually got the role.

e. Whitey admits that times he "stretches the truth just a jot—for the sake of color."

---

9. a. According to Tom Wolfe's essay "King of the Status Dropouts," Playboy magnate Hugh Hefner has seventeen clubs with membership numbering more than a half-million.

b. Hefner owns two foreign holdings, a club in Jamaica and another—featuring gambling—on London's Park Lane.

c. Hefner leased the Palmolive Building in Chicago and has converted it into the Playboy Building.

d. Hefner is having a Los Angeles apartment built that features indoor swimming pools, sauna baths, and revolving walls that convert rooms into bars.

e. He began this empire with $600 of his own money and $2,000 that he had borrowed.

---

10. a. In 1925, when General Billy Mitchell was convicted of insubordination by a U.S. Army court-martial, the only member of the board who disagreed with the "guilty" verdict was General Douglas MacArthur.

b. Mitchell had incurred the wrath of powerful officers when he proved in an actual test that a battleship could be sunk by aerial bombing, and he further angered them by telling the press how little foresight the "old-line" brass had.

c. Just prior to his dramatic demonstration of air power, Mitchell had been quoted as saying, "The General Staff knows as much about the air as a hog does about skating."

d. The year before his court-martial, Mitchell had publicly predicted with uncanny accuracy the 1941 bombing of Pearl Harbor by the Japanese, who were ostensibly friendly toward us in the 1920's.

e. Even after he quit the army to avoid being ejected, Mitchell barnstormed around the country speaking on behalf of air power and the need to be prepared.

EXERCISE 14: *Make a single sentence out of each of the following groups of sentences. The finished sentence should have one main clause and as many subordinate elements as you need to include all the details. Place the most significant element of each group in the main clause of your finished sentence.*

Example

Original: Larry Nugent is a man who believes strongly in the virtues of physical toughness. Nugent recently parachuted into Lake Tahoe with a group of Marines.

48

Revision: *Because* he believes so strongly in the virtues of physical toughness, Larry Nugent recently parachuted into Lake Tahoe with a group of Marines.

1. *A Clockwork Orange* is a movie. It is based on a novel by Anthony Burgess. Many readers of the book were very doubtful that it could be made into a successful movie.

_____

_____

_____

2. Holy man Nashpur Karamcheti collected five hundred rupees from a crowd. The crowd had gathered to see him walk on the Ganges. A moment later he sank to the bottom.

_____

_____

_____

3. Occasionally things happen that we can't explain with our present knowledge of natural laws. We call such things "supernatural." Sometimes we ridicule or deny these occurrences.

_____

_____

_____

4. Keith Moran occasionally goes on week-long hunger strikes. He goes on a one-week hunger strike whenever he has an argument with his wife. His wife is a very tyrannical woman.

_____

_____

_____

5. Clarence Darrow was a famous lawyer. Clarence Darrow didn't believe that teaching Darwin's theory of evolution to American youth could corrupt them. He defended teacher John Scopes, who was tried for "godlessness" in the famous "Monkey Trial" of the 1920's.

_____

_____

_____

6. Everyone warned Guy Fawkes that blowing up Parliament would be dangerous. They said he would have a hard time if he were caught. Guy Fawkes tried it anyway.

_____

_____

_____

EXERCISE 15: *Combine the short sentences in each of the following paragraphs into one long sentence. The long sentence should have a main clause and as many subordinate clauses or phrases as you need to include all the details. The main clause of each revised sentence should relate to the TS. Place one line under the subject and two lines under the verb in each revised sentence.*

Example

TS: Skiing can be a hazardous sport.
Original: Fred Pebble is from Long Beach, California. Pebble is a lawyer. He went skiing at Lake Arrowhead. Lake Arrowhead is in the San Bernardino Mountains. Pebble tried a dangerous slope. Pebble broke his left ankle.
Revision: Long Beach lawyer Fred Pebble broke his left ankle when he tried a dangerous ski slope at Lake Arrowhead in the San Bernardino Mountains.

1. TS: Great athletes often succeed in spite of their handicaps.
   Original: Jesse Owens' legs were injured. His legs were severely injured. Owens' legs were injured in a childhood accident. He won four gold medals. He won them at the Olympics. The Olympics were held in Berlin in 1936.

   Revision: _____

   _____

   _____

   _____

2. TS: Elmo Whipple finally went too far with the foreman.
   Original: Elmo Whipple has herded cattle for Alf Hanson for twenty-five years. Whipple told Hanson's foreman, Grubb Phillips, that Phillips didn't know a steer from a musk ox. Whipple was fired.

   Revision: _____

   _____

   _____

3. TS: The local elementary school punished nonconformity recently.
   Original: Dolores Haze is a sixth-grader. She attends La Lolita Elementary School. She was expelled from school. Her expulsion took place yesterday. She was expelled for coming to class in a bathing suit. This was in violation of the dress code.
   Revision: _____

   _____

   _____

4. TS: The state finally ended the disturbances caused by motorcycle gangs.
   Original: The members of one gang call themselves the "Filthy Few." They terrorized the town of El Burrito. El Burrito is in New Mexico. The New Mexico highway patrol surrounded them in a saloon. The highway patrol took them into custody.
   Revision: _____

   _____

   _____

5. TS: A new weather prophet caused southern California doctors to work overtime last weekend.
   Original: Emma Lavinia Hopewell is spiritual leader of a religious group. The group is called the Children of the Flame. Thirty-seven members were hospitalized for sunstroke recently. They had stood in the desert for seven hours waiting for their leader to bring rain.
   Revision: _____

   _____

   _____

6. TS: The town critic finally earned himself some grief last month.
   Original: Pop Higgins never misses a chance to criticize the civic leaders. Pop publicly described the mayor of Middletown as being "several bricks short of a full load." The mayor is Art Primrose. Primrose sued Pop for slander.
   Revision: _____

   _____

   _____

7. TS: In a novel by Joseph Conrad, the character Charles Marlow represents common sense and sanity in a chaotic world.

Original: Charles Marlow is a sea captain. In the novel *Heart of Darkness*, he patches up the pipes of his leaky old steamboat. He does this so that the steamboat can continue its trip. The steamboat is making a rescue trip up the river. It's the Congo River. Everyone else aboard the steamboat is running about in confusion.

Revision: _____

_____

_____

_____

8. TS: Benvenuto Cellini is an example of an artist who had extremely destructive tendencies.

Original: Benvenuto Cellini was a fifteenth-century Italian. He was a Florentine. He was a sculptor. He was also a lover. He killed more than ten opponents in rapier duels. He left us one of the world's most famous biographies.

Revision: _____

_____

_____

_____

9. TS: Graduates today sometimes accept employment that is less challenging than what their schooling prepared them for.

Original: Byron Bunkwork is an ambitious young man. He holds a master's degree in comparative literature from Yale. He works at a carwash. The carwash is in Worcester, Massachusetts. There are no teaching jobs available.

Revision: _____

_____

_____

_____

10. TS: Like Emily Dickinson, author Joyce Carol Oates believes that "the soul selects its own society."

Original: Joyce Carol Oates was recently interviewed. She said that our meaningful relationships with others are complex. Throughout our lives, each of us encounters only a small number of people who have a lasting effect on us.

Revision: _____

_____

_____

_____

EXERCISE 16: *Do exactly as you did in the preceding exercise.*

1. TS: Judging from recent transactions, it would seem that artists aren't always poor.

   Original: Andrew Wyeth is fifty-six years old. He is from Chadds Ford, Pennsylvania. He recently sold a painting entitled "Her Room." It was sold for $65,000. This sale price establishes a record for an American artist during his own lifetime.

   Revision: _____

   _____

   _____

   _____

2. TS: The underworld becomes more ingenious all the time.

   Original: A group of thieves discovered some rare gems in the Egyptian Museum. They discovered the gems last month. The gems were valued at $5,000. The thieves got the gems out of the museum by washing them down a drainage pipe in the washroom and catching them in a screen about a mile from the museum.

   Revision: _____

   _____

   _____

   _____

3. TS: The nation's most publicized lovers are discreet about their plans.

   Original: Jet-setters Lavonia Nemwitz and Cesar Barranca faced the press in Acapulco, Mexico. Lavonia is twenty-two years old. Barranca is twenty-seven years old. They denied rumors that they were going to be married. They claimed they were merely taking a vacation in Acapulco.

   Revision: _____

   _____

   _____

   _____

4. TS: Pablo Casals is noted for his religious devotion.

Original: The Archbishop of San Juan, Puerto Rico, said a special mass for Pablo Casals. Casals is a famous cello player. Casals was celebrating his nine-tieth birthday. The musician wept as the mass was offered.

Revision: _____

_____

_____

_____

5. TS: For some students, English composition can be a disappointment.

Original: Laszlo Tibor is from Hungary. Tibor worked at least four hours a night on English. He received special help from his instructor. Tibor failed English 1 for the second time.

Revision: _____

_____

_____

_____

6. TS: Lumir Zampach is a master of trickery.

Original: Lumir Zampach is an American agent of Czech descent. He once fooled Russian train guards. It was on a train traveling through Czechoslovakia. Zampach dressed himself as a conductor.

Revision: _____

_____

_____

_____

7. TS: The teaching philosophy of some professors stresses student discipline.

Original: Martin Bratwurst teaches economics at Heidelberg University. He once told a student that five hours of outside study was required for every hour spent in class. Bratwurst said that the student's absolute commitment to the subject was to be taken for granted.

Revision: _____

_____

_____

_____

8. TS: Cecilia Selkirke is a woman who prides herself on her faithfulness to her husband.

  Original: Cecilia Selkirke is a secretary with the Cooper Copper Company. She is an attractive woman. Her boss, an affectionate man, repeatedly asks her to sit on his lap. She adamantly refuses because she is married.

  Revision: _____

          _____

          _____

          _____

9. TS: College students often stand up in vain for their principles.

  Original: Michael Monmouth attends El Borracho State College. Michael Monmouth is a sophomore. Michael is nineteen years old. He staged a five-day fast to protest the governor's cutbacks in educational appropriations. He received no publicity for the protest. He forgot to inform the press.

  Revision: _____

          _____

          _____

          _____

10. TS: Actions speak louder than words.

  Original: George Bilkwood is a corporation executive. George lives next door to me. He has been claiming for years that he's a better singer than Frank Sinatra. He failed to make the choir at the Presbyterian church.

  Revision: _____

          _____

          _____

          _____

EXERCISE 17: *Read each of the following paragraphs for unity. After deciding what the main (or controlling) idea of the topic sentence is, check the independent clause of each subsequent sentence against that controlling idea. If you find sentences that are not directly related, rewrite them so that they are subordinated to an independent clause that does relate to the TS.*

1. (1) On the basis of Gregorio Panatela's performance in the past seven fights, boxing experts and fans alike judge him to be the world's most effective welterweight. (2) In March, Panatela went to Chicago to fight fourth-ranked Delbert Brooks. (3) He knocked Brooks out with a left hook in the final minute of the seventh round and earned a place among the top ten welterweights. (4) Three weeks later, Panatela went to New Orleans for a ten-round bout. (5) Though he fought with an injured left hand, he out-pointed number one contender Archie Ponchatrain at the Municipal Stadium. (6) Panatela waited four months before flying to Lima to fight Peruvian welterweight champion Bartolo Ledesma. (7) He knocked Ledesma out at the beginning of the seventh round. (8) Last month he was in New York to face world champion Harvey Bromo in a nontitle ten-rounder at Madison Square Garden. (9) Panatela won a clear-cut decision after staggering Bromo twice. (10) He staggered the champion in the second round and again at the beginning of the ninth. (11) These victories over the short span of one year have earned Gregorio Panatela the title "The Uncrowned Welterweight King."

2. (1) During Hitler's 1938 inspection of Italy's assets, Mussolini practiced his famous gift for creating the grand illusion. (2) Hitler's party was taken in a motorcade through certain streets. (3) These streets had been redesigned to look like movie sets. (4) Hitler viewed only pleasant, clean little communities. (5) He didn't know that just behind the façade lay squalor. (6) Hitler had traveled by train from Brenner to Rome. (7) The houses along the route had been patched up and given fresh coats of paint. (8) It gave the illusion of a thriving Italy. (9) Shortly afterwards, Hitler reviewed the vaunted Italian army. (10) The troops he saw were tall, blue-eyed men. (11) They had been chosen specially to give the impression that Italians, like Germans, were "Aryans." (12) Although the same men had been shifted from one spot to another ahead of the Führer, Hitler thought he was reviewing different troops each time. (13) All this was done to create the illusion of great numbers. (14) Ultimately, Mussolini's misrepresentation of Italian grandeur may have contributed to the defeat of the Axis powers.

3. (1) Though he was eager to succeed in college, Mike Dylan experienced various disappointments during his first four weeks at Cerebros. (2) During the first week he faithfully attended the lectures on composition, even though he failed to understand the explanation of topic sentences and found the concept of unity completely baffling. (3) On Wednesday evening of the third week he went to the library to study Gibbon's *Decline and Fall of the Roman Empire*. (4) He got into an intimate discussion with a brunette cheerleader, neglected Gibbon, and subsequently failed the following morning's history quiz. (5) He thought he understood his Chemistry 1 assignments. (6) However, by the end of the third week his instructor suggested that he drop the course while he still could. (7) On Thursday of the fourth week, in Miss McNeill's composition class, he wrote what he would have sworn was a unified paragraph. (8) He was told the following Monday that his paragraph did not count toward his grade.

4. (1) M. Diana Delacy, a young assistant professor of English, is unsparing in her criticism of graduate students. (2) Dr. Delacy teaches at Brookdale University in Lodi, California. (3) She described one graduate student's classroom presentation as "a skillful song and dance." (4) Another student had been teaching in the public schools for six years. (5) Dr. Delacy evaluated him with the statement, "The superficiality of his paper on Steinbeck was exceeded only by the shallowness of his presentation of the subject to the class." (6) She added, "For that matter, Steinbeck is shallow, too." (7) A third student was a young woman. (8) Her paper dealt with the subordinate role of women in nineteenth-century English literature. (9) Professor Delacy gave the paper a C. (10) She argued that the thesis was untenable and the whole paper thus invalid. (11) Dr. Delacy, who received her Ph.D. from a prestigious university, is fond of saying, "Grad students here at Brookdale would have lasted a week at Stanford. So did Steinbeck."

3
Coherence

As we have been insisting, unity is a basic structural component of good writing. As such, it must be present in any piece of prose worth reading. However, unity alone—without the help of certain other qualities—cannot ensure a successful paragraph. Consider the following example:

> (1) Old Man Suggins is the meanest man in Northfork. (2) He beats his wife once a week. (3) His kids always have bruises on their cheeks. (4) He burned down old Elmer Combine's outhouse because Elmer couldn't pay back a three-dollar poker debt. (5) Old Man Suggins turpentined our dog Effie last May Day. (6) He said he had his reasons for doing it. (7) That's pretty rank, don't you believe?

This paragraph certainly has unity—all the facts relate to the idea that Old Man Suggins is the meanest man in Northfork. But in this case, unity alone is not enough to make the writing good. The prose is choppy and abrupt. There are no transitions between individual sentences. The paragraph seems to need some words or phrases or signals to ease the movement of the prose and make the separate facts stick together. This quality, which is present when individual elements stick together, is called *coherence*. It's the companion of unity. It's the glue that joins the ideas together.

As you remember, unity deals with the relationship between the topic sentence and each of the sentences that follow. Coherence involves the relationship that occurs from sentence to sentence within the paragraph. These sentences must flow together, must be woven together much as a fine piece of fabric must be smoothly knit. We don't expect to find snags, tears, and protruding threads in an expensive piece of cloth. Similarly, good prose should be free of awkward sentences and bumps in the writing. Consider the following student paragraph, which, in the quality of its content, is one cut above the preceding example:

(1) It has become obvious that Senator F. Garth Doolin III is taking advantage of his political position for personal gain. (2) One transgression was financing thirty-three personal trips with tax money. (3) Many senators questioned the need for a tour of Africa. (4) Doolin had charged it to an expense account. (5) His ex-wife complained of not receiving her alimony; he admitted to endorsing the checks himself and placing them in the bank. (6) Doolin has acquired a certain notoriety in his home district for escaping payment of a $25,000 court award. (7) He has avoided it by going home only on Sundays. (8) Skeptical onlookers are beginning to wonder whether he can remain in office. (9) One typical Doolin supporter put it this way, "Quit gripin', man. That guy Doolin's a swinger!"

The writer of this paragraph obviously knows what he's talking about. Its content, of course, is superior to that of the opening paragraph on Old Man Suggins. The writer of the paragraph about Senator Doolin has taken the trouble to get the facts, and he has unified these facts. But after all that effort, he undermines the effectiveness of what should have been a fine paragraph. He allows his sentences to bump along in a staccato way, when he could have smoothed out the writing with very little effort. He sacrifices ease in his writing by neglecting coherence. To avoid such pitfalls yourself, you can achieve coherence in a number of ways.

Transition

The most convenient way of smoothing gaps in prose is through *transition*, a term that comes from the Latin *transire*, meaning "to go over or across." Most people would probably agree that it's more pleasant to cross chasms by bridges than by trying to leap over (much safer too!). Like bridges, transitions open into two directions at the same time—forward to where the writer intends to go and backward to where he has been. Transitions most often are indicated by single words or short phrases, which can generally be positioned almost anywhere in a sentence. The following transitional words and phrases occur most frequently in writing:

To signal an addition:	and, furthermore, besides, next, moreover, in addition, again, also, similarly, too, finally, second, subsequently, last
To signal an example or illustration:	for example, thus, for instance, that is, namely
To signal a contrast or alternative:	but, or, nor, yet, still, however, nevertheless, on the contrary, on the other hand, conversely, although

To signal a conclusion: therefore, thus, then, in conclusion, consequently, as a result, in other words, accordingly, finally

Let us see if the paragraph on F. Garth Doolin might be improved if we used some transitional phrases.

It has become obvious, *finally*, that Seantor F. Garth Doolin III is taking advantage of his political position for personal gain. One transgression, *for example*, was financing thirty-three personal trips with tax money. Many senators questioned the need for Doolin's tour of Africa. Doolin had charged it to an expense account. When his ex-wife complained of not receiving her alimony, *moreover*, he admitted to endorsing the checks himself and placing them in the bank. *Besides all this*, Doolin has acquired a certain notoriety in his home district for escaping payment of a $25,000 court award. *Apparently* he has avoided settlement by going home only on Sundays. *Consequently*, skeptical onlookers are beginning to wonder whether this man can remain in office. *Yet* one typical Doolin supporter may have voiced the sentiments of the district. "Quit gripin', man," he advised. "That guy Doolin's a swinger!"

Repetition

An equally important though less obvious method of achieving coherence is through repetition of and reference to key words in the paragraph. Often these words are pronouns, but they may be nouns and sometimes adjectives as well. For our purposes, nouns and pronouns are probably best. The student can no doubt see the reason why pronouns—words that are "stand-ins" for nouns—are particularly useful in linking ideas from sentence to sentence. They establish a pattern of identity running through the paragraph by referring back to nouns or to other pronouns that precede them. These words keep the reader's attention focused continuously on the people, objects, or ideas that are the subject of the paragraph. Consider whether the coherence of our sample paragraph is further improved by the following repetition of key terms or substitutes for those key terms:

It has become obvious, finally, that Senator F. Garth Doolin III is taking advantage of *his* political position for personal gain. One transgression, for example, was *his* financing thirty-three personal trips with tax money. Many senators questioned the need for Doolin's tour of Africa. Doolin had charged *that venture* to *his* expense account. When *his* ex-wife complained of not receiving *her* alimony, moreover, *he* admitted to endorsing *her* checks *himself* and placing *them* in *his* Washington bank. Besides all this, Doolin has acquired a certain notoriety in *his* home district for having escaped payment of a $25,000 court award. Apparently *he* has avoided *that* settlement by going home only on Sundays. Consequently, skeptical onlookers are beginning to wonder whether *this man* can remain in office. Yet one *typical Doolin supporter* may have voiced the sentiments of the district. "Quit gripin', man," *he* advised. "That guy Doolin's a swinger!"

Modification

Modification is another method of improving coherence in prose. To modify something means to change it in some respect. The enthusiast who modifies a stock-car engine, for instance, alters the standard specifications of that engine, hopefully in such a way that it has more power and thus can produce greater speed. In modifying his prose, a writer tries to give it more power by adding details to individual sentences. Most often, these details enhance the quality of the writing by contributing *specific* pieces of information that the reader wants to know. Modifiers answer such questions as *who, how, when, where, why,* and *under what circumstances.*

Modifiers come in many varieties. They can take the form of single words, such as adjectives or adverbs:

Adjective: an *impressive* congressman
Adverb: a *vitally* important law
Adjectival past participle: a *forged* document

These modifiers tend to affect the power of the nouns they modify. The modifier in the first instance announces that the congressman is impressive rather than simply identifying his profession. In the second example, *law* (a neutral enough noun) becomes both important and vital after modification. In the third example, the document becomes an illegal one.

Modification can also be accomplished with phrases. The three most common types of modifying phrases are:

A. Past participial:
1. *Forged by the counterfeiters*, the check was soon revealed to be worthless.
2. The check *forged by the counterfeiters* was soon revealed to be worthless.

B. Present participial:
1. *Printing checks to their hearts' content*, the counterfeiters hoped to swindle every bank in town.
2. The counterfeiters, *printing checks as rapidly as possible*, hoped to swindle every bank in town.

C. Prepositional:
1. *After wrecking their press*, the counterfeiters decided to skip town.
2. The counterfeiters, *after ruining their plates*, decided to skip town.
3. The counterfeiters decided to skip town *after running into some bad luck.*

Note that the modifying phrases used above provide information about the crime. That is, the phrases *modify* the original situation by telling *who* in example **A**, *how* in example **B**, and *when* in example **C**. Note also that all these modifiers can be used at several places in the sentence.

Of the three types of phrases, the prepositional phrase is the most useful and versatile. It conveys a wide range of information without cluttering up the sentence.

The counterfeiters printed the money (at their hideout) (in an old warehouse) (on Ruskin Street).

In the above example, the three successive prepositional phrases tell *where* the counterfeiters operated. In the following sentence, prepositions tell *when, why, how,* and *where*:

> *In November* the counterfeiters, *in order to buy Christmas gifts*, printed the "tens" *on a new press in their hideout on Ruskin Street.*

Let us look at our sample paragraph once more to determine if adding some modification will improve its coherence:

> It has become obvious, finally, that Senator F. Garth Doolin III is taking advantage of his political position for personal gain. One transgression, for example, was his financing thirty-three trips to *Caracas, Venezuela, from Washington* with tax money. Many senators questioned the need for Doolin's tour of Africa. *Accompanied by a pretty secretary and a female corporation lawyer*, Doolin had charged that venture to his expense account. When his ex-wife complained of not receiving her alimony *of $20,000*, moreover, he admitted to endorsing her checks himself and placing them in his Washington bank. Besides all this, Doolin has acquired a certain notoriety in his home district of Williamsport for escaping payment of a $25,000 court award *to Mrs. Madeline Bragg for slander.* Apparently he has avoided that settlement by going home only on Sundays, *at which time he enjoys immunity from the courts. In the light of all these revelations*, skeptical onlookers are beginning to wonder whether this man can remain in office. Yet one typical Williamsport voter may have voiced the sentiments of the district *concerning Doolin's behavior.* "Quit gripin', man," the voter advised. "That guy Doolin's a swinger!"

Notice how, in addition to improving coherence, the above modifications help flesh out the prose by contributing information. We learn such things as *where* those tax-supported trips were taken, *who* went along, *how much* the alimony amounted to, *why* the Senator was being sued, and by *whom.*

Logical Order

Modification can also be put to special uses in the paragraph. One such use that should be important to the serious student of writing is the establishment of *logical order* in the paragraph. Logical order helps to keep writing coherent because it ties the ideas to a distinct structure: time, space, or cause and effect, to mention a few possibilities. Before we take leave of Senator Doolin and his problems, let's look at the paragraph for one last time; now we will establish a *chronological* (time) *order* by using certain kinds of modifications:

> It has become obvious, finally, that Senator F. Garth Doolin III is taking advantage of his political position for personal gain. One transgression, for

example, was his financing thirty-three trips to Caracas, Venezuela, from Washington with tax money *during the current session. Earlier in the year,* many senators questioned the need for Doolin's tour of Africa. Accompanied by a pretty secretary and a female corporation lawyer, Doolin had charged that venture to his expense account. *More recently,* when his ex-wife complained of not receiving her alimony of $20,000, moreover, he admitted to endorsing her checks himself and placing them in his Washington bank. Besides all this, Doolin has acquired a certain notoriety in his home district of Williamsport for escaping payment of a $25,000 court award to Mrs. Madeline Bragg for slander. Apparently he has avoided that settlement, *over the past two years,* by going home only on Sundays, at which time he enjoys immunity from the courts. In the light of all these revelations, skeptical onlookers are beginning to wonder whether the Senator can remain in office. Yet one typical Williamsport voter *last week* may have voiced the sentiments of the district concerning Doolin's *future.* "Quit gripin', man," the voter advised. "That guy Doolin's a swinger!"

You may be likely to object at this point that the paragraph is "overdone." Perhaps it is. But if there is exaggeration here, it is meant to illustrate those subtleties in writing that lie hidden within the texture of the prose. These modifications aren't supposed to stand out, since good writing doesn't call attention to itself but rather to the subject it treats. Yet the student must deliberately try to see how these devices work before he can employ them himself.

EXERCISE 18: *After reading the following paragraph, answer the multiple choice questions at the end of the selection. When required to fill in blanks within the paragraph, choose the appropriate answer from the list given in the multiple choice section.*

(1) Certain authorities on human behavior claim that the costumes people wear to parties provide subtle insights into their personalities. (2) San Francisco psychiatrist Dr. Francis J. Rigney, for instance, suggests that the most timid guests arrive costumed in a conventional manner through fear of self-expression. (3) This sort of person will attend a Halloween party as a ghost or will arrive at a pirate party safely disguised as Long John Silver, complete with peg leg. (4) Bolder guests may think they are creating a whimsical or daring image when actually they are revealing aspects of themselves that they'd rather not admit existed. (5) The woman who arrives dressed as innocent Little Miss Muffet, _____ , may be expressing an unconscious desire to retreat from womanhood, while another woman who comes portraying Raquel Welch may actually be sexually repressed. (6) According to psychologists, the most uninhibited guests will deliberately and sometimes daringly express their true personality through a carefully planned disguise. (7) Such people might appear in the guise of a historical personage whom they admire and perhaps resemble in certain respects. (8) Very seldom will they dress as animals or criminals but instead will wear costumes that display a healthy degree of self-esteem. (9) _____ they also have the freedom of personality to wear costumes that reflect a sense of humor about themselves.

(10) _____ , they too, like the others, accepted the invitation to attend a costume party.

1. In sentence 2, the expression "for instance" is an example of:
   a. subordination
   b. transition
   c. modification
   d. repetition
   e. logical order
2. Choose the following transition that best fits the blank in sentence 5:
   a. of course
   b. next
   c. moreover
   d. for example
   e. nevertheless
3. Choose the following transition that best fits the blank in sentence 9:
   a. subsequently
   b. lastly
   c. yet
   d. namely
   e. secondly
4. Choose the following transition that best fits the blank in sentence 10:
   a. still
   b. conversely
   c. accordingly
   d. however
   e. after all
5. In sentence 10, the pronoun "they" refers back *ultimately* to which of the following antecedents?
   a. "they" in sentence 9
   b. the women discussed in sentence 5
   c. "such people" in sentence 7
   d. "uninhibited guests" in sentence 6
   e. "animals or criminals" in sentence 8
6. The phrase "This sort of person" in sentence 3 is an example of:
   a. transition
   b. modification
   c. repetition
   d. logical order
   e. subordination
7. The phrase "through fear of self-expression" in sentence 2 is an example of:
   a. transition
   b. modification
   c. repetition
   d. logical order
   e. subordination

8. Which of the following best describes the type of logical order employed in the paragraph?
   a. time
   b. space
   c. moving from most timid to least timid
   d. cause and effect
   e. moving from least timid to most timid
9. In sentence 6, the phrase "According to psychologists" is an example of which of the following?
   a. transition
   b. modification
   c. repetition
   d. logical order
   e. subordination
10. In sentence 7, the phrase "Such people" is an example of which of the following?
    a. transition
    b. modification
    c. repetition
    d. logical order
    e. subordination

EXERCISE 19: *Do exactly as you did in the preceding exercise.*

(1) Not many American success stories can match the 1925 rise to fame and fortune of Illinois' Harold ("Red") Grange. (2) The big ballyhoo that characterized his senior year began after a November 2 football game when Grange was carried two miles on the shoulders of his peers. (3) Later that autumn, Grange's campus admirers circulated a petition nominating the twenty-two-year-old halfback for Congress of the United States. (4) _____ did Grange lack opportunities to earn big money. (5) _____ _____ , he enjoyed the luxury of refusing a $40,000 contract that the New York Giants offered him for his services in just three late-season pro games. (6) Ignoring the Giants completely, Grange _____ accepted an offer from the Chicago Bears who agreed to pay him $12,000 just to put his name on paper and an additional $30,000 for his first day's work, a game to be played on December 6 in New York. (7) Even the movies wooed Red; a company called the Arrow Picture Corporation, now extinct, signed him to a contract on December 7. (8) Socially speaking, the highlight of the year came the very next day when Grange was introduced to President Calvin Coolidge in Washington. (9) _____ despite all the hoopla of the football season, Grange's public image turned out to be—as always with images—a fleeting thing. (10) Just five years after his season of fame, "The Galloping Ghost" was reported to be working for small wages in a Hollywood night club.

1. The phrase "after a November 2 football game" in sentence 2 is an example of:
   a. transition
   b. repetition

c. modification

d. subordination

e. logical order

2. Which of the following transitions best fits the blank in sentence 4?

   a. and

   b. when

   c. then

   d. nor

   e. next

3. Which of the following transitions best fits the blank in sentence 5?

   a. then

   b. in fact

   c. next

   d. perhaps

   e. however

4. In sentence 6, the phrase "Ignoring the Giants completely" is an example of:

   a. transition

   b. repetition

   c. modification

   d. pronoun reference

   e. logical order

5. Which of the following transitions best fits the blank in sentence 6?

   a. therefore

   b. consequently

   c. yet

   d. in addition

   e. finally

6. The phrase "called the Arrow Picture Corporation" in sentence 7 is an example of:

   a. transition

   b. repetition

   c. modification

   d. subordination

   e. logical order

7. Which of the following transitions best fits the blank in sentence 9?

   a. now

   b. moreover

   c. consequently

   d. finally

   e. yet

8. "The Galloping Ghost" in sentence 10 is an example of:

   a. transition

   b. repetition

   c. modification

   d. subordination

   e. logical order

9. The phrase "the football season" in sentence 9 refers back to:
   a. "the year" in sentence 8
   b. "that autumn" in sentence 3
   c. "senior year" in sentence 2
   d. "1925" in sentence 1
   e. all the above
10. The logical order maintained in the paragraph might best be described as:
   a. space
   b. cause and effect
   c. time
   d. moving from least to most significant
   e. both c and d
   f. both a and b

EXERCISE 20: *Fill in each blank with the transitional or modifying expression that is best suited to the meaning of the paragraph.*

1. _Although_ Mrs. George W. Clark of Hampton, Virginia, had heard nothing from her prisoner-of-war son for three years, she did not contact the Committee of Liaison with Families of Servicemen Detained in North Vietnam, _apparently_ _____ an FBI agent had warned her against doing so. The FBI agent appeared unexpectedly at her home in October 1970, presented his credentials, _____ _and_ told her that the committee was linked with the Communists and _furthermore_ its information was undependable. _When_ Mrs. Clark and her husband told him they had heard nothing from their son through Red Cross or direct mail channels, he _moreover_ _again_ warned her not to go to the committee _but_ he gave her no other reasons. This left the Clarks pretty desperate _because_ the committee has been the only group able to maintain correspondence between American prisoners in North Vietnam and their families at home. The matter, _however_, has not ended there. _When_ members of Congress heard Mrs. Clark's story, a House Foreign Affairs Subcommittee demanded the retirement of J. Edgar Hoover, _and_ Congressman Jonathan Bingham of New York told Mrs. Clark to go ahead and seek the liaison committee's help.

2. Among the panelists at the 138th national meeting of the American Association for the Advancement of Science were Ralph Nader; Anthony Massocchi of the Oil, Chemical and Atomic Workers International Union; Dr. George A. Wald, a Nobel laureate from Harvard, who chaired the meeting; and Dr. Sidney Wolfe of the National Institute of Health. _Although_ men of entirely different professions, "all the panelists agreed that the importance of health hazards in industry has been largely ignored or underemphasized by government, union, and management." Nader said that the subjection of workers to the dangers of industrial poisons is the "worst dimension" of our ecological problem. _Later_ Wald said that _even though_ death rates from a number of industrial diseases are appallingly high, science has paid little attention to them. Wald _then_

said that _furthermore_ about "6,000 poisonous chemicals are now used in industry, and 600 new ones are added every year, only 450 of these are covered by federal safety standards." _And_ the deaths go on: 4,000 a year in the coal mines from pneumoconiosis (black-lung disease), byssinosis (brown-lung disease) among workers in textile mills, silicosis among workers in plants crushing sand or stone or glass, and asbestosis, _which_ "bloodies the lungs of asbestos workers exposed to the mineral's needle-sharp fibers." _However_, although the Occupational Safety and Health Act was passed in 1969, only "5,000 of the 4.1 million dangerous work places in America" have been checked since then, _according_ to Wolfe. And, _although_ the government lists 14,000 industrial-accident deaths a year and 2.5 million disabling injuries, _both_ Wolfe and Wald agreed that the figures are "grossly underestimated."

3. Over the past eight months, several events have established Buck Shawnley as the most controversial student body president in the history of OCJ. _As can be suppos_ Shawnley ran as a write-in candidate on a platform that opposed "city hall and the status quo on all issues, both great and small." _Accordingly_, after he was elected, Shawnley began to scrap openly with the board of trustees and the administration over the college dress code, which, he claimed, "perpetuated adolescent dependency and aborted individuality." The new president _in addition_ used the college radio station to publicly censure the local voters, who had defeated a bond issue designed to gain funds for seminars on "everything from zither-playing to quoit-tossing." _Nor_ did Shawnley spare the press, which he claimed "went out of its way to establish long hair on young men as the mark of the deviant, the unestablished, the resentful, and the untrustworthy." With all the adverse publicity he has received, Shawnley _apparently_ regards the time he has spent as president as "a productive and happy chapter of my life."

EXERCISE 21: *Fill in each blank with the transitional expression that best expresses the logical relationship between the sentences.*

1. Hartley was short and homely, with a beaklike nose and a receding hairline. He had a bad temper, and he never missed a chance to cruelly embarrass his dates. _____ most of the women in our high school class were dying to go out with him.
2. Evolution has gifted today's mammals with a high metabolic rate and the capacity to maintain a constant body temperature. _____ mammals are not a prey to the temperature of their immediate surroundings and have a much greater ability to adapt than cold-blooded animals like reptiles and amphibians.
3. The high mammalian metabolic rate does not come without its price, _____, for a heavy intake of food is constantly required to sustain it.
4. The human brain at birth is about 330 cubic centimeters in size, not much larger than a baby gorilla's. _____ by the time both gorilla and man are mature, the man's brain is at least twice as large as the gorilla's.

5. Sir Garth Bridgeport is a scholar and a member of the Royal Society for the Advancement of Science. He is a distinguished racing-car expert, having designed the car that won last year's *Mille Miglia.* _____ , he is a champion chess-player and a fine polo-player.
6. Anton Ristic spent ten years at forced labor in a Soviet mine just south of the Arctic Circle. It is understandable _____ that he still suffers from frequent nightmares.
7. Everyone became pretty frustrated after the rain had continued without letup into the twenty-seventh day. But, _____ , toward noon of that day the sun appeared for the first time in nearly a month, and the rain stopped.
8. Frostley doesn't indulge in smoking, drinking, or gambling. _____ is it likely that he'll ever succumb to those vices.
9. After twelve hours of deliberating, the jury had come to no decision regarding Martin Milobar. _____ Judge Ripstitch called for a recess until the following day.
10. There is one man and one man alone who could possibly speak without interruption for that length of time, _____ , Fidel Castro.

EXERCISE 22: *Sometimes the sentences in a paragraph are "glued" together so well that even when their order is deliberately scrambled, as it is below, a reader can rearrange them as they were in the original paragraph. Indicate the correct order of the sentences on the blank below. Circle the words that do the "gluing" job.*

1. (a) Nationwide publicity led to a role in a third-rate Hollywood movie, *Good Times with a Bad Girl,* that went on to enjoy considerable commercial success. (b) When nude modeling proved more lucrative and less tiring than dancing, Vivian posed for the now-famous calendar that quickly turned up on the walls of diners and garages throughout the Southwest. (c) Grasping the significance of Vivienne's effect on audiences, Hollywood producer Hirschfield Melrose cast her opposite Vicente Salce in *Azusa Afternoons,* a controversial film that critics said would probably establish Vivienne as the reigning sex-goddess of the American cinema. (d) Fame sometimes comes quickly to those who possess a certain personal magnetism. (e) The resultant regional public exposure drew the attention of *Playboy,* which featured Vivian in their summer centerfold as Vivienne D'Angere, a name she felt might better serve her ambitions. (f) Vivian Matarazza graduated from being head drum majorette at a Phoenix high school to dancing topless-a-go-go in Tucson.

Correct order: _____

2. (a) Huge "Truth" signs, reiterating the message of the buttons, preceded every entourage of party officials and flanked all their speakers. (b) "Truth must go much deeper than the mere image of truth," said their leader, Congressman Gideon Bible. (c) Above all else, the founders of the Universal Party strove to create the impression of complete truth. (d) On desks in every precinct office from New York to

Pacificville, smaller signs—instead of reminding people to "Think"—ordered party workers to "Tell the Truth." (e) So dedication to total truth, it must be said, was the platform of the new party. (f) "It must be so pervasive," he went on, "so clearly the basic motivation behind everything we do, that no other image could be possible." (g) Finally, all over the nation—at every intersection, at every crossroad, on every byway, highway, and freeway—automobile bumper stickers exhorted Americans to "Follow the Truth." (h) To endorse Bible's words, "Truth" buttons of a dozen different colors (blue predominating) adorned the clothes of all party leaders and their supporters.

Correct order: _____

3. (a) He enforces the laws with undeviating severity while the Duke masquerades as a lowly friar. (b) Through one of Shakespeare's wrong-girl-in-the-right-bed plots, Isabella preserves not only Claudio's life, but her own honor. (c) It is a play about honor that is marked by the lack of it: the lovers are mostly lechers, and purity is mocked as pretense. (d) In a fury of purity, Angelo orders a young gentleman, Claudio, to be executed for fornication. (e) *Measure for Measure* is one of Shakespeare's sour comedies. (f) Suddenly his puritanical iciness melts into lust, and he offers Isabella her brother's life in exchange for her body. (g) Claudio's sister Isabella, a novice in religious habit, pleads with Angelo to show mercy. (h) Concerned with the state of public morals, the Duke of Vienna selects Angelo, a man of seemingly flinty virtues, to take full power over the state.*

Correct order: _____

EXERCISE 23: *Do exactly as you did in the preceding exercise.*

1. (a) In between are several other varieties, including the small car, the American compact, the standard family sedan, and the American luxury car. (b) At one extreme is the limousine, which may appear to be a half-block long. (c) Cars now come in a bewildering variety of sizes. (d) At the other extreme is a vest-pocket foreign car that sometimes gives the impression that it could be wound up with a key.

Correct order: _____

2. (a) Others write in their revisions between the lines, in the margins, or in the blank spaces at the top or bottom of the page. (b) Different writers use different methods when they revise their work. (c) And yet others staple their insertions to the sheets containing their earlier versions. (d) Some careful writers retype their work completely every time they revise it. (e) Still others are cut-and-paste experts; they physically cut out unwanted material and paste in little pieces of paper with new material.

Correct order: _____

---

*Adapted from "The Theater: Mocking Bird" *Time* (February 24, 1967). Reprinted by permission from TIME, The Weekly Newsmagazine; Copyright Time, Inc., 1967.

3. (a) Perhaps someday he will have an electronic device that automatically types out what he says, when he says it. (b) Today man may write with a regular pencil, a mechanical pencil, a fountain pen, a ball point pen, or a typewriter. (c) Throughout history man has used a wide variety of instruments for writing. (d) Medieval monks often employed a quill to draw inked lines on parchment, a specially processed leather made from sheepskin. (e) Some ancient peoples used a sharp pointed stylus to cut lines on layers of wet clay, which later dried into bricklike tablets.

Correct order: _____

4. (a) Lemming's first role at the Pasadena Playhouse as Biff in *Death of a Salesman* made him known to theater fans throughout Southern California and earned him favorable reviews in the trade papers. (b) In his eighth-grade play in Eau Claire, Wisconsin, Houston Lemming gave a performance of the Tin Woodsman in *The Wizard of Oz* that people still talk about. (c) Nearby Hollywood soon tapped his talent for the role of Sugar in Sam Sagonis' *Dreamer with a Thousand Faces,* which was an enormous success at the box office. (d) The senior plays at Eau Claire High School featured Houston Lemming in the lead roles in Shakespeare's *King Lear* and *As You Like It.* (e) Back on the West Coast, Houston received $25,000 per episode in his successful TV series *Ramsey,* in which he played a relaxed but heavy-fisted private detective. (f) During his hitch in the Army, Houston's perform-ances as modern dramatic heroes and antiheroes gained him coverage in *Stars and Stripes.* (g) At the University of Wisconsin, he gained campus fame for his portray-als of Lennie in the stage adaptation of John Steinbeck's *Of Mice and Men* and the Gentleman Caller in Tennessee Williams' *The Glass Menagerie,* his first attempts to enact distinctly modern stage heroes. (h) The stage version of *Dreamer* played for fifty weeks to full houses at New York's Lincoln Center, with Houston drawing critical praise for his portrayal of Sugar.

Correct order: _____

5. (a) Things really began to get desperate when Dean Gradgrind placed all "question-able" textbooks on a prohibited list subject to examination by a community board of elderly ladies. (b) The dean then extended the Friday workday until 9:30 P.M. with the institution of Friday evening classes. (c) The clincher came when the dean was named president for the coming year, on which occasion he decided to dismiss seven "defiant" English instructors. (d) In just one year as Dean of Instruction at Milkweed, Dr. Josiah Gradgrind has managed to alienate the entire faculty. (e) The situation worsened at midyear, when the dean refused to extend any support what-soever to an English instructor who had been attacked by an adult student for "stressing a foul word" in J. D. Salinger's *Catcher in the Rye.* (f) Dr. Gradgrind first instituted compulsory attendance at weekly departmental meetings in order to "in-sure a cohesive spirit in keeping with the impressive tradition of Milkweed College."

Correct order: _____

EXERCISE 24: *The words in each of the following lists can be grouped into separate categories on the basis of association. After you have set up different categories, try to establish a logical order for the words within each of the categories. Use your own paper for this exercise.*

1. Hannibal, afternoon, near, Alexander, morning, Napoleon, evening, far, Westmoreland, Sheridan, there, Custer, Patton, night, Pershing, here, Attila
2. brave, mayor, illness, prudent, citizen, pentagon, president, virus, cowardly, triangle, governor, rectangle, weakness, circle, convalescence, recovery
3. Buchanan, precipitancy, elation, Kennedy, procrastination, serenity, Nixon, punctuality, Madison, Garfield, depression, morbidity, gladness, haste
4. excellence, affection, ineptitude, dislike, capability, tolerance, incompetence, love, mediocrity, passion
5. pope, priest, recruit, college president, lieutenant, dean, cardinal, instructor, bishop, colonel, department head, corporal, student, general, layman, chief-of-staff

EXERCISE 25: *This is an exercise to help you understand the use of repetition in a paragraph. Each of the underlined words is followed by a word or phrase that refers to it. Circle every word or phrase that refers to the underlined word, and draw a line connecting the word or phrase with its antecedent.*

(1) People held in servitude have been identified by various names throughout history. (2) Slaves, of course, were literally the personal possessions of their masters, who often held life and death powers over them. (3) Scarcely more privileged than slaves were vassals in medieval England and France, who received land from their feudal lords in return for homage, allegiance, and hard and arbitrary labor. (4) Unlike slaves, vassals did not owe their bodies and souls to their lords without promise of recompense; in actuality, however, their lot was often little better than that of the slaves. (5) In Latin America, the peon, like the vassal, was bound in service to a landlord creditor, who could often extract from his "debtor" enormous labor, as well as portions of all crops grown on the land. (6) Russia and Eastern Europe had their serfs, workers who were bound to the land and governed by a lord. They could not vote, were denied most basic human rights, and could be conscripted arbitrarily into military service. (7) The indentured servant of colonial America was under contract to work for a specified length of time in return for his passage to the New World and his room and board once he arrived. (8) His contract often failed to protect him from mistreatment, although it did fix the date of his release from his obligation. (9) Whatever its degree, its name, or the location where it was practiced, servitude has always equaled human bondage, and modern men everywhere justly fear and revile it.

EXERCISE 26: *The following paragraphs show how coherence is achieved through the use of devices that link one idea to another. Moving from sentence to sentence, analyze the devices used for achieving coherence in these paragraphs. Be prepared to discuss your findings in class.*

1. (1) Julius Fast, in his book *Body Language*, tells us that there are many "alphabets" of body movements which, when viewed by a perceptive onlooker, say more about us than words could. (2) Many of these "alphabets" belong to traditional and systematized performances. (3) Mime troops, for instance, enact sophisticated cultural commentaries that are understood completely by experienced audiences. (4) In Hawaii, hula dancers narrate complete traditional tales with their hands, and their gestures are understood perfectly by other members of their culture. (5) According to psychologists, masking actions used by people to conceal their feelings are a less conspicuous form of the body movement alphabet. (6) Every teacher knows that students often sit through dry academic lectures looking alert and bright-eyed while secretly watching the clock. (7) In many instances, a guest at a boring party hides his discomfort by smiling a lot and exchanging inane chatter. (8) But still subtler are the small body messages each of us sends more or less unconsciously in acting out our emotional state. (9) For example, we raise an eyebrow to reveal our disbelief, rub our nose when we're puzzled, tap our fingers when impatient, and avert our eyes when embarrassed. (10) To the experienced or intuitive observer, a person's every movement conveys its own meaning more honestly than a verbal declaration.

2. (1) Domestic water supplies in Japan have become so badly polluted that many people install water purifiers in their homes or buy bottled mineral water to drink. (2) The government has reported that even the water in rural areas has become polluted; prior to this, polluted water had been found only in metropolitan areas. (3) The government report says that in 1964 there were only sixty-nine known cases of major water pollution, but by 1969 the number had more than doubled. (4) Because many cases have not been reported, the government believes that the real number is much higher. (5) The increase in the amounts of purifying chemicals used in municipal water supplies is also evidence of the rapid increase in pollution. (6) A typical case is that of the Tama River in western Japan, in which the amount of chemicals necessary to neutralize the poisons in the water has increased by 500 percent in recent years. (7) Although Japan's water was once clean and pure, factory wastes, agricultural chemicals, and sewage have made it unfit for drinking everywhere except in the mountains, near the sources of lakes and rivers. (8) At the moment, the principal substitute for the polluted drinking water is mineral water, but it has become nearly as expensive as saki.

4
Support

You probably recall our promise to discuss the subject of support in writing. Good writing must have concrete support, just as a bank must have sufficient capital. After all, facts, ideas, and illustrations are the writer's stock in trade, the coin he works with. Without authentic material to back it up, writing has no value. Poor writing is, in fact, a declaration of bankruptcy. The following student paragraph, despite certain unity and coherence, has no real content. There is no money in this bank:

(1) For a beginning freshman, college is no easy thing. (2) It's very difficult, especially after high school, where you weren't given much responsibility. (3) Everything was cut and dried, and you had to do it. (4) But in college nobody forces you to do anything. (5) You just wake up one day and know you flunked. (6) That's what is so hard about college—having to do it on your own. (7) Nobody likes to have to suddenly shift for themselves. (8) Moreover, it's difficult to develop responsibility after being taken care of all your life by parents and teachers, and responsibility is a long process. (9) This is why college is tough for freshmen. (10) I know, because I flunked out after the first semester.

It should be obvious to you that if this student doesn't put some *content* into his writing, he is probably heading for a repeat performance of his first semester.

To stay in business as a college student, you must take the trouble to get the facts. No one is interested in reading a series of generalizations; it's too hard for the reader to relate them to his own life, to his own situation in the world. Writing takes on interest for the reader as it becomes *concrete*. Consider, for example, the fables of the Greek storyteller Aesop. Each tale serves to point up a moral or a bit of wisdom. You'll recall that in the story of the town mouse and the country mouse, two rodents travel to the home of the town mouse in search of a more luxurious way of life. But when they sit down to the leavings of a penthouse feast, they are frightened away by the dogs of the house. The tale ends with a message: better beans and bacon in peace than cakes and ale in fear.

The wisdom of Aesop's judgment about life is driven home by the *specifics*, by the details of the story itself. No one would be particularly happy to hear the moral repeated over and over again without the story. Your writing must combine specific facts with generalizations. For the present, you should try to concentrate more on detail than on generalization in your writing.

Specific Support

Perhaps the use of specific detail can best be illustrated by another paragraph about the freshman's academic problems:

> (1) For the new freshman, adjusting to the discipline that college study demands is no easy matter. (2) Most difficult, perhaps, is accepting increased responsibility for unsupervised work. (3) In our English 13 class, for instance, a day-to-day journal was assigned in the first week, and no more was said about it for a month. (4) Suddenly, in the fifth week, Mr. Brimstone called for the completed journals, penalizing all students whose journals were incomplete. (5) One must also face the necessity of devoting many hours to study outside of class. (6) On the first day of school, the orientation instructor pointed out that in many classes at least two hours of outside study were required for every hour spent in class, and this turned out to be a conservative estimate. (7) I found, for example, that it took me an entire weekend to read even a book as interesting as John Steinbeck's *The Grapes of Wrath*. (8) The student must also face such minor problems as having classes that meet only twice a week instead of every day, as in high school. (9) In such a case, the student sometimes tends to get "cold" in the four-day period between Thursday and the following Tuesday. (10) It becomes clear to me that President Stonehenge may have been right when he said in the opening speech to the freshmen, "Shake hands with the person on your left and then on your right. By the end of this semester only one of them will still be here."

You will probably find the above paragraph more convincing than the first one cited in this chapter. Undoubtedly, your increased interest results for the writer's use of specific content rather than generalizations. Notice the kind of facts that the writer uses. In sentence 3, for instance, we learn the specific name of the class, *English 13*—not "my English class" or, worse yet, "in one class." We find out in the same sentence that the assignment was made the *first week*, and in the following sentence we learn that the journals were requested in the *fifth week* by *Mr. Brimstone*—not just "the teacher." Sentence 6 contains several specifics: *first day of school, two hours for every hour spent in class*. Sentence 7 contains the title of a book and the name of its author. Sentence 9 mentions the specific lapse of time occurring between classes. The concluding sentence contains an actual quotation—which is a very concrete type of support—

and the name and position of the person making the statement. If you don't believe that it is the factual quality of the paragraph that improves the writing, consider what happens if we eliminate a few specific details. Let's leave out the quotation and the president's name:

> It becomes clear to me that our college president may have been right when he said that only one out of three of us freshmen would still be around by the end of the first semester at this college.

How much less personal and dramatic this sentence becomes when the direct quotation and the speaker's name have been omitted! It's still somewhat factual, of course, but some of the life has been drained from it. An appropriate quotation, strategically placed, adds authentic detail and human interest to a piece of prose.

Perhaps at this point you think that most of what we're saying sounds all right in theory, but that professional writers probably don't make a federal case out of using specifics. For the hardened cynic, the following paragraph might illustrate how an experienced professional *does* use details:

> (1) Russell Train, chairman of the White House Council on Environmental Quality, believes that the U.S. can at least start lessening its energy problem right now by reducing waste. (2) "We must shift our thinking from simply finding more energy sources to concerning ourselves with how to use energy more efficiently," he says. (3) With better technology, most appliances can be made to consume less power and throw off less heat. (4) The common light bulb uses only 10% of the electricity it burns, for example, and refrigerators can easily be produced to use 50% less power. (5) More important, there is plenty of room for improvement in methods of generating and transmitting electricity. (6) One remedy is an advanced but until recently neglected system with the awesome name of magnetohydrodynamics. (7) MHD can produce electricity directly from the high-velocity flow of hot, ionized gases, with 60% efficiency instead of the present 35%. (8) Similarly, superconductive, supercold (-320° F.) power lines can cut transmission losses. (9) Though both technologies are costly, they would yield much more power per unit of fuel with less pollution.*

The writer of the paragraph above has satisfied the reader's curiosity about the possibilities of conserving natural energy that is apparently now being wasted through faulty or inefficient technology. In sentence 2 he introduces a speaker by means of a quotation. Direct quotation renders "expert" opinion more convincing and is a dramatic means of imparting the quality of the spoken word to a piece of writing. In sentence 4 the writer identifies the items he has in mind in sentence 3 when he mentions "appliances"—light bulbs and refrigerators. The introduction in sentence 6 of the transmitting system called MHD and the citation of the percentage of efficiency increase that MHD would yield are also important to the discussion of energy conservation. The use of details in the writing keeps the reader interested while it performs its major function—keeping the reader informed.

*From "Energy Crisis: Are We Running Out?" *Time* (June 12, 1972). Reprinted by permission from TIME, The Weekly Newsmagazine; © Time Inc. 1972.

Biographical writing also benefits by the inclusion of detail. The following paragraph deals with Detroit pitcher Mickey Lolich's frustrating failure to achieve the stature his talent deserves:

> (1) Lolich grew up contrary, but if he had not, baseball might well have made him so. (2) For nine years he has been one of the game's outstanding pitchers. (3) But like Lou Gehrig, who labored first in the shadow of Babe Ruth and then Joe DiMaggio, Lolich has usually seemed to be second best. (4) He had the initial misfortune of being teamed with the Peck's Bad Boy of baseball, Denny McLain. (5) The outstanding performance of Lolich's career—three World Series victories over the St. Louis Cardinals in 1968—was virtually lost in the glare of McLain's 31 victories that season. (6) In 1971, Lolich won 25 games and struck out 308 batters, tops in either league. (7) He also pitched 376 innings (the most by a major league hurler in 55 years) and threw 29 complete games (the most by an American League pitcher since 1946). (8) So who won the 1971 Cy Young Award as the league's outstanding pitcher? (9) Oakland's highly publicized Vida Blue.*

In the above paragraph the author, aware that this is a nation that loves statistics, frequently makes use of numbers as a type of support. The writer's comparison of Lolich with other past and present major leaguers, who are identified by name, also lends authenticity to the writing. Once again, the writer has taken the trouble to be specific, and has satisfied the reader's curiosity about Mickey Lolich and his elusive goals.

Sources for Specifics

Where does one find these concrete, specific details that we've said provide substance in a piece of writing? Actually, there is more in the world to write about than most people think there is. For instance, metropolitan newspapers are a daily and inexhaustible depository of facts. Some students have even been known to use advertisements as a source of detail. Books, especially nonfiction, are often filled with material that could be adaptable to your paragraphs. Among nonfiction sources, biography and autobiography are especially rich in specific detail and have the added advantage of dealing with human nature, always an interesting subject. But as the paragraph on Mickey Lolich suggests, perhaps the richest source of such information is a weekly newsmagazine such as *Time, Newsweek,* or *U.S. News and World Report.*

As a compilation of useful details, a weekly newsmagazine commends itself in several respects. For one thing, the information is current, and everyone is interested in what is happening *now.* More significantly, it is highly factual in content, if at times biased in its selection of some facts and its omission of others, as we'll try to indicate in examples. Its most valuable feature, however, is its use of generally the same kind of paragraph structure that we'll be advocating through this book: strong topic sentences at the beginning supported by specific details and followed by a concluding or transitional

*From "Fat Man on the Mound," *Time* (June 19, 1972). Reprinted by permission from TIME, The Weekly Newsmagazine; © Time Inc. 1972.

sentence that usually summarizes the main idea of the paragraph and prepares us for the next.

But how does one properly use the details found in a newsmagazine? Perhaps the best way to answer that question is to demonstrate step by step what one student did in constructing a paragraph out of facts he found in a *Time* magazine article. The following is a *Time* article entitled "Fortress California."

As you read this article, try to surmise what *you* would do with it if you were asked to summarize it in one paragraph.

Sir Edward Coke, the keenest legal mind of the 16th century, first laid down the principle that a man's home is "his castle and fortress, his defense against injury and violence." Sir Edward was speaking figuratively, of course, but now it appears that many Americans are taking him literally. The National Commission on the Causes and Prevention of Violence, taking note of the rapid rise in urban crime, not long ago made a grim prediction: "high-rise apartment buildings and residential compounds protected by private guards and security devices will be fortified cells for upper-middle and high-income populations." The fortifications are already appearing across the land, most notably in California (where burglaries have increased by 149% in the past decade) and particularly in the southern part of the state, where Los Angeles County suffers the nation's highest suburban crime rate.

By the latest count, there are at least three dozen walled "total security" communities in the desert, beach and woodland areas of Southern California, and more are on the drawing boards. "Until about five years ago," says Los Angeles County Deputy Planning Director Frederick Barlow, "most subdividers wanted the county to maintain their streets. Now a majority of the subdivisions we are approving have private streets" (which entitles the communities to block off the streets with gates and guards).

Typical of the walled communities is a 200-house complex called The Shores in Laguna Niguel, north of San Diego, where many of the armed guards at the gatehouse are ex-Marine combat veterans of the Viet Nam War. "More than likely, the presence of a guard cuts out a lot of crime." understates John Rogers, a burly guard. Nearby Rossmoor Leisure World, in Laguna Hills, is a retirement community surrounded by six-foot-high pink walls and guarded by a security force of 170 unarmed resident patrolmen led by four armed professionals. They man the community's eight carefully guarded gates and patrol its streets round the clock in radio cars.

Some of the newer walled communities are installing remarkably sophisticated security systems. The Mission Hills condominium in the desert near Palm Springs is being rigged with electronic Westinghouse units that monitor for fires, burglaries or equipment failures. Signals are fed to a local computer center that alerts firemen, police or maintenance men and, in addition, activates a net of ultrasensitive microphones installed inside each house, allowing a dispatcher to listen in while help is on the way. Residents are enthusiastic. "I feel so good when I know that I'm entering a house that is untouched," says a Mission Hills housewife.

Another guarded community, 125-home Westlake Island, north of Los Angeles, is reachable only by bridge. A guard inspects visitors at the entrance to the bridge. checks with the resident to be sure that company is expected, and only then allows the guest to drive across the moat. As a result, the island is crime-

78

free. "The biggest problem we have," says one guard, "is keeping sightseers off the island and breaking up teen-age parties that get out of hand." Each home-owner on the island pays an annual $220 assessment (nondeductible) covering the cost of the guards and general upkeep, but Islander Walter Smith, robbed twice in his previous flat, thinks the price is a bargain. "I always used to keep a loaded gun by the bed in our Beverly Hills apartment," he says, "but now I don't give it a thought." Rumors about the surrounding waters may contribute to the islanders' sense of security. "Some people claim there are crocodiles in there," jokes Airline Pilot Richard Neet. "The water is better than a wall," says his wife, Ellie; "I don't feel claustrophobic here."

Water does not always guarantee security. Even Westlake Island could learn something from an exclusive, 21-home development in Florida's Hobe Sound, which uses the Westinghouse system with an added touch: because the commu-nity is built along a network of canals, a closed-circuit television system monitors the waterways to keep amphibious thieves away.*

The following paragraph was based on details taken from the *Time* article:

(1) Although protecting one's property from theft today is often accomplished through technology, some of the oldest means of security known to man are be-ing updated and used to protect planned communities. (2) Many of these deter-rents go as far back in history as does man's need to guard his possessions. (3) Rossmoor Leisure World in Laguna Hills, California, for example, is a compact, modern version of the old walled city, complete with a private army of sentries patrolling its six-foot enclosure and guarding its eight gates. (4) Westlake Island near Los Angeles is encircled by a medieval-style moat and is accessible only by means of a guarded bridge, obstacles that keep the community free from invasion by thieves and vandals. (5) So while gadgets such as closed-circuit television sys-tems and ultrasensitive microphones are frequently used to guard the new com-munities, many of the most popular security methods actually date back to antiquity.

The writer of the above paragraph obviously was able to choose from the article the details he wished to focus on and to arrange those details into a meaningful working order. Let's trace the method he used to write his paragraph. He began by considering a number of possibilities for the main idea of the paragraph.

First possibility:	Focusing on the national crime problem reflected in the reference to the National Commission's prediction.
Decision:	There seemed to be too little information about crime on either a national or state level. The article mentions only one crime statistic (in Los Angeles) and two states. More limitation of the subject is needed.
Second possibility:	Focusing on a description of the communities where secu-rity is so highly-prized and the main type of security used there.

*"Fortress California," *Time* (May 1, 1972). Reprinted by permission from TIME, The Weekly Newsmagazine; © Time Inc. 1972.

Decision: Such an approach could lead to a simple listing of locations and a description of the main means of security employed in the communities under discussion. This might be better than the first alternative above, but perhaps the writer can better focus his subject by thinking about some other possibilities as well.

Third possibility: Focusing on the traditional means often used to ensure security in modern planned communities. The writer also touches in a subordinate way on the modern technological devices used for security.

Decision: This seems the most promising approach to writing a paragraph based on the article "Fortress California" without simply imitating the article. The writer imposes his own imagination on his writing—the comparison of the new American communities with the armed strongholds of the past. This approach allows him to play off the old against the new to a modest extent.

Now let's examine the steps the writer took in organizing the paragraph.

1. First he tried a tentative topic sentence:
   Security methods in new communities combine the old and the new.
2. The writer defined the key thought in the topic sentence as *security methods combine old and new.*
3. The rest of the paragraph must support and develop that idea.
   a. Walls and patrols represent the old.
   b. Moats and bridges represent the old.
   c. Closed-circuit television systems and ultrasensitive microphones represent the new. (This detail is correctly subordinated in both the TS and in sentence 5.)
4. The writer knows that in order to give fullness to the writing he must do more than simply list old ways and new ways. He decides to stress one in favor of the other. His belief in the value and effectiveness of the older methods is emphasized when he places the mention of them in the *main* or *independent* clause of his topic sentence.
5. Notice: While using the material contained in the article, the writer has worked out a theory of his own: He suggests subtly that the new and technically complex does not always render the traditional obsolete. He uses imagination in comparing some communities to ancient walled cities, others to fortresses defended by moats. None of these comparisons was made explicitly in the article.
6. By changing his tentative topic sentence to the version appearing in the finished paragraph, the writer broadens and expands his entire concept to include the playing-off of the technological against the traditional.
7. He chooses an appropriate ending—one that relates to the topic sentence but is not simply a repetition of the topic sentence.

In the construction of this paragraph, the writer has made a generalization from a group of specific details. Then he has turned around and supported the generalization with those details. Note that the paragraph does not have the strict main clause unity we stressed so much before. Yet it does not sacrifice a singleness of purpose. By this point in the course, you may be ready to take the responsibility of maintaining unity without making each main clause agree with the controlling idea, so long as your paragraphs—like the one above—demonstrate a clear singleness of purpose. Perhaps you could also find your own approach to the facts you are interpreting. The above writer seems to suggest that the new and the traditional can be successfully combined, and he suggests it without altering the facts.

Separating Fact from Opinion

By this time we have harped so much on the value of factual, specific support (as opposed to generalization) that we've surely become bores. Try to hang on as we attempt to make a final, clear distinction between a fact (sometimes called a "report") and an opinion (sometimes called a "judgment" or "interference"). Check the differences between the following sets of facts and opinions:

Opinion	Fact
Annette Spumoni is a lovely girl.	Annette Spumoni has an oval face, even features, blue eyes with heavy lashes, a brilliant smile, a rosy complexion, and shiny black hair.
Jason Wampum is a wealthy, powerful man.	Senator Jason Wampum's assets include a yacht valued at $150,000, two high-rise apartment buildings on Chicago's Lake Front, and a string of restaurants along the Pacific Coast.
By all the laws of chance, Japan's Pearl Harbor attack should never have succeeded.	In December 1941, the Japanese navy crossed the North Pacific at its stormiest season with a huge, conspicuous task force. It was spotted before the attack at least twice by civilian pilots. The force was also picked up by American radar but ignored.

As can be seen, facts are verifiable, objective statements based on measurement and observation. Any two of us looking at Annette Spumoni would probably agree that she has an oval face and blue eyes, because we are members of a culture in which there is a consensus as to what shape *oval* describes and what shade constitutes the color *blue*. Regarding Annette's loveliness, however, observer A may disagree with observer B, since standards of loveliness tend to be a matter of individual taste. Thus, a *matter of fact* can be settled fairly impartially, but a *matter of opinion* often cannot, for an opinion is a statement of an attitude toward a set of facts; hopefully, that opinion is based on facts or details. There are valid opinions and invalid ones. Do not assume from what we've been saying that facts are somehow more valuable than opinions. It is true that in a court of law, facts are generally required in proof or disproof of testimony. But opinion, especially if it is expert opinion, is also valued when it can be established that the opinion is soundly based.

A good paragraph has a high ratio of facts to generalizations. A generalization is made in the topic sentence and repeated in the primary support, which is discussed in the next chapter. But the secondary support—the real substance of the paragraph—is long on fact and short on opinion. Consider the following extract from an essay. We will then try to make a distinction between fact and opinion. Remember, we are recommending that you extract the *facts* from a piece of prose, not that you borrow its opinions or imitate the style of the wording. We don't want you to be guilty of copying from a book or a magazine. However, facts are public property once they have been published.

(1) Hefner has had the publicity and financial success to compete for status at the highest level. (2) And yet the whole thing has been somehow *infra dig* by orthodox, European-style, Eastern status standards. (3) First of all, Hefner is completely Midwestern. (4) He was born in a God-fearing but socially only fair-to-middling family in Chicago. (5) He went to the University of Illinois. (6) His first and only marriage—he was separated in 1954, divorced in 1959—was not "social." (7) But mainly the source of his money has always carried a taint in traditional status terms: *Playboy*, a "skin magazine," as they say at Yale, and the Playboy Clubs, "those Bunny houses."

(8) Worse still, he accomplished it all in Chicago, if one can imagine that. (9) And even Chicago has been a little frosty about it. (10) The Chicago *Daily News* recently published a list called "The 62 Best People in Chicago." (11) This amounted to a status roster based not only on ancestry and corporate rank but on recent accomplishment. (12) Almost anyone of any prominence in Chicago made it, but Hugh Hefner did not, despite the fact that he is perhaps the most successful entrepreneur Chicago has had since 1945 and certainly the best known.

(13) Hefner has been the most successful new magazine publisher since World War II. (14) He started out with $600 of his own money and $2,000 he borrowed and now has a business that grosses $48 million a year. (15) *Playboy* magazine's circulation keeps going up, from 742,000 in 1956 to 1,117,000 in 1960 to 1,877,000 in 1963 to almost 4,500,000 currently. (16) Three-fourths of it is newsstand sales, which is the most profitable kind of circulation to have. (17) Convincing people to subscribe and then mailing the magazine out to subscribers is expensive. (18) *Playboy* sells for 75 cents a copy and does something no other slick magazine can manage; namely, it turns a profit on newsstand income all by itself. (19) Hefner claims that all the advertising revenue is gravy, pure profit, and it is prodigious, up from $8 million in 1964 to an estimated $17 million for 1966.*

Let's examine the factual content of the above writing and distinguish it from opinion. The numbers below refer to the sentences in the quoted selection.

1. Hefner has had the publicity and financial success to compete for status at the highest level.	Opinion and generalization. This opinion is so demonstrable that it tends to take on the nature of fact.

*Reprinted with the permission of Farrar, Straus & Giroux, Inc. from *The Pump House Gang* by Tom Wolfe. Copyright © 1968 by Tom Wolfe, copyright © 1966 by the World Journal Tribune Corporation, copyright © 1964, 1965, 1966 by the New York Herald Tribune, Inc.

2. The whole thing has been *infra dig* by orthodox, European-style, Eastern status standards.	Opinion and generalization. This is less readily demonstrable *factually* than sentence 1. It has a higher element of personal opinion.
3. Hefner is completely Midwestern.	Fact in the sense that he was born and reared in the Midwest. Opinion in the sense that it implies a judgment about Hefner's personal style.
4. Born in a God-fearing but socially fair-to-middling Chicago family.	Fact: Hefner was born in Chicago. Opinion: His family was socially modest and conventionally religious.
5. Went to the University of Illinois.	Fact.
6. First and only marriage—separated 1954, divorced 1959—not a "social" marriage.	Fact: His first and only marriage ended in separation in 1954 and divorce in 1959. Opinion: the marriage was not "social."
7. Source of his money has always carried a taint in traditional status terms: Playboy a "skin magazine," says Yale, and clubs "Bunny houses."	Opinion: that his source of wealth is not esteemed among traditionalists. Some fact occurs after the colon. We can assume that someone at Yale called *Playboy* "a skin magazine" and the clubs "Bunny houses."
8. Worse still, he accomplished it all in Chicago.	Opinion: the writer's wry attitude toward Hefner's chances of making a fortune in Chicago is obvious.

The third paragraph has one opinion (the topic sentence, number 13), which is supported in every succeeding sentence by factual material: statistics, monetary figures, an indirect claim by Hefner that the advertising in the magazine yields pure profit. In paragraph 2, we find a blend of fact and opinion. The list the author mentions was actually published in the Chicago *Daily News*. It was a list based on recent accomplishments. Hefner was not on it. Perhaps this fact tends to underscore some of the writer's generalizations about Hugh Hefner made in the first paragraph of the excerpt. All these factual details could be used by a student writing a paragraph about a man's rise to power in magazine publishing.

Let's review the ways for establishing concreteness and factuality in a piece of writing. These methods include the use of the following:

1. Simple statistics concerning a person's background—when he was born, where he comes from, where he lives, where he has been.
2. Quotations—direct or indirect—with the identification of the people who made them.
3. References to actual publications where pertinent information about the subject appeared: "The 62 Best People in Chicago," a list published by the Chicago *Daily News*.
4. Historical events that figure in the treatment of a subject: World War II.

Avoiding Plagiarism

A constant danger in using facts from any source is that you will plagiarize, which means copying verbatim or even paraphrasing too closely what is found in an original source. To avoid plagiarism, try following these practical suggestions:

1. If you use a fact or facts from a source, name the source in your paragraph (or in a footnote if you are writing a heavily documented paper).
2. More important, reword the factual statement in your own vocabulary. Do not lift the statement in its exact wording from its source.
3. Avoid using the same descriptive words (verbs, as well as adjectives and adverbs) that are found in the original text. Look out for emotionally loaded words, such as scrambled, thrust, blasted, cheated, hostile, brutal, exterminated, sterile, violent, honest, and so on.
4. Avoid restating the writer's opinions. Develop your own opinions based on the facts.
5. If you do use the writer's opinions, be sure to distinguish clearly between his opinions and your own, and between facts and opinions in your source.

The following passage has been excerpted from George Orwell's essay "Reflections on Gandhi." After you have studied the excerpt and the student's paragraph that follows it, you should have a better understanding of what constitutes plagiarism and should be able to avoid it in your own writing.

However, Gandhi's pacifism can be separated to some extent from his other teachings. Its motive was religious, but he claimed also for it that it was a definite technique, a method, capable of producing desired political results. Gandhi's attitude was not that of most Western pacifists. *Satyagraha,* first evolved in South Africa, was a sort of non-violent warfare, a way of defeating the enemy without hurting him and without feeling or arousing hatred. It entailed such things as civil disobedience, strikes, lying down in front of railway trains, enduring police charges without running away and without hitting back, and the like. Gandhi objected to "passive resistance" as a translation of *Satyagraha*: in Gujarati, it seems, the word means "firmness in the truth." In his early days Gandhi served as a stretcher-bearer on the British side in the Boer War, and he was prepared to do the same again in the war of 1914–18. Even after he had completely abjured violence he was honest enough to see that in war it is usually necessary to take sides. He did not—indeed, since his whole political life centered around a struggle for national independence, he could not—take the sterile and dishonest line of pretending that in every war both sides are exactly the same and it makes no difference who wins. Nor did he, like most Western pacifists, specialize in avoiding awkward questions. In relation to the late war, one question that every pacifist had a clear obligation to answer was: "What about the Jews? Are you prepared to see them exterminated? If not, how do you propose to save them without resorting to war?" I must say that I have never heard, from any Western pacifist, an honest answer to this question, though I have heard plenty of evasions, usually of the "you're another" type. But it so happens that Gandhi was asked a somewhat similar question in 1938 and that his answer is on record in Mr. Louis Fischer's *Gandhi and Stalin*. According to Mr. Fischer, Gandhi's view was that the German Jews ought to commit collective suicide, which "would have aroused the world and the people of Germany to Hitler's violence." After the war he justified himself: the Jews had been killed anyway, and might as well have died significantly. One has the impression that this attitude staggered even so warm an admirer as Mr. Fischer, but Gandhi was merely being honest. If you are not prepared to take life, you must often be prepared for lives to be lost in some other way. When, in 1942, he urged non-violent resistance against a Japanese invasion, he was ready to admit that it might cost several million deaths.*

Now let us consider a student's paragraph based on George Orwell's paragraph:

(1) Although Gandhi's pacifism resembles that of many Westerners, it differs from it in several very important ways. (2) Like many Westerners' pacifism, its motive was religious, and it was used as a means of achieving good political results. (3) But Gandhi believed in *Satyagraha*, a sort of nonviolent warfare, which "involved civil destruction, strikes, getting in the way of railroad trains, sustaining police charges without running or striking back." (4) In the Boer War Gandhi was a stretcher-bearer on the side of the English and was ready to do the same again for the British in the First World War, and even after he came out against violence, he was honest enough to see that in war it is usually necessary to take sides. (5) He did not take the sterile and dishonest line of believing that all wars are the same and that it doesn't make any difference who wins. (6) Also, unlike most Western pacifists, he never forgot that under some forms of oppression and tyranny great numbers of people might be killed even if they did not resist—witness annihilation of the Jews during the Second World War. (7) According to Louis Fischer, Gandhi said that the German Jews should have committed collective suicide. (8) This would have called the world's attention to their troubles, and it didn't make any real difference because they were all killed anyway. (9) This way, at least, their deaths would have had some significance. (10) In 1942, he urged nonviolent resistance against the Japanese invasion of India. (11) He said it might cost several million deaths. (12) So you can see how Gandhi's pacifism is different from most Westerners'.

To examine briefly for plagiarism: The underlined words in sentences 2, 3, 4, 5, 7, 8, 10, and 11 are Orwell's, not the student's, and the student has used them without giving Orwell credit through the use of quotation marks. In sentence 3 the quotation is not verbatim and hence inaccurate. Remember, all quotations must be exactly the same as they were in the source. In sentence 4 the student presents Orwell's opinions as if they were his own. They might well be his own, but Orwell stated them first, and he must be given credit for them. This is easy to do: Use "According to Orwell," "Orwell says," "Orwell believes," or something of that sort, and you are covered. Without doing that, you are plagiarizing another man's thoughts. In addition, sentence 4 contains plagiarized words and structures. In sentence 5 the structure and, again, many of the words are Orwell's, but no credit is accorded him. Complete the analysis of the

*From *Shooting an Elephant and Other Essays* by George Orwell, copyright 1945, 1946, 1949, 1950, by Sonia Brownell Orwell. Reprinted by permission of Harcourt Brace Jovanovich, Inc.

paragraph yourself. Study each sentence separately and see how many examples of plagiarism you can find and define.

The principal origin of the plagiarism in the student paragraph is in the writer's failure to give us his own mental reaction to Orwell's work. He is merely attempting to paraphrase the passage. Because the student was writing primarily from Orwell's page rather than from his own mind, Orwell's thoughts, words, and structures automatically came tumbling out onto the student's page. The following paragraph is the student's final version, in which he made an effort to give his opinions of the facts and ideas rather than Orwell's.

(1) According to Orwell, Gandhi's pacifism was quite different from the pacifism of most Westerners. (2) A follower of *Satyagraha*, the Indian name for Gandhi's form of pacifism, does take sides. (3) He does not use physical violence, but he resists aggression in various other ways. (4) He takes the side of the people he agrees with, and from that position he faces the enemy. (5) He deliberately gets in their way; he says "no" whenever he can. (6) He will choose to starve or maybe even be shot down rather than submit, and in his own way he will give the enemy plenty of trouble all the time. (7) To me this is more courageous and honest, if you are a pacifist, than just saying, "all quarrels and wars are lousy and, therefore, I won't take sides." (8) But I think Gandhi realized that in some cases many people might die if they practiced nonviolent resistance. (9) He said, for example, that the German Jews should have "committed collective suicide" as a form of protest. (10) Well, as terrible as that sounds, I agree that it would have had more meaning than not resisting at all and yet dying anyway. (11) Although I personally sympathize with most American pacifists, I would agree with both Orwell and Gandhi that any pacifist who says that all wars and all sides are equally evil has not thought very deeply about his pacifism.

Whatever the shortcomings of this paragraph, it is honest, and it is the result of some thinking on the student's part. He has not simply repeated Orwell's ideas, words, and grammatical constructs. This paragraph is acceptable, whereas the one before it is not, because it is free of plagiarism. Anyone who makes use of outside sources to obtain information for his writing must make a constant effort to avoid plagiarism. It isn't wrong to rely on what you read. You have every right to increase your knowledge by consulting outside sources for information, but in using that material in your writing, you must find your own words, style, and thoughts.

Summary

1. Good writing is a combination of opinion and fact, but practically speaking, more fact than opinion is desirable in most student writing.
2. Topic sentences convey an opinion that most of the remaining sentences support factually.
3. Specifics (concrete items) include such things as numbers, names, titles of works, statistics, quotations, and the narration of events that took place.
4. Useful sources of specific details include newspapers, biographical and nonfictional works, newsmagazines, textbooks, and one's own observations.

5. Fact deals with what actually occurred or exists; opinion makes a judgment concerning that actual occurrence or state of being.
6. Cite your source somewhere in your paragraph.
7. Above all, any material that you use must be expressed *in your own words* and not in the words of a professional writer. Base your own opinions on the facts. Come to your own conclusions regarding the facts.

Facts are the *substance* of a piece of writing—the marks of its authenticity. You can't write convincingly unless you have something to write about. Maybe even old Aesop would agree with us when we conclude with a moral of our own:

You can't make chicken salad out of feathers.

EXERCISE 27: *In the blank preceding each of the following statements, write F if the statement is fact or O if it is an opinion.*

_____ 1. Americans are essentially an idealistic people who tend to take their democracy straight.

_____ 2. Despite the appearance of an occasionally sincere and just objector, the antiwar movement is characterized by massive immaturity.

_____ 3. Near Agra in northern India, a man named Goonga charges onlookers five rupees in return for performing a 170-foot dive into a reservoir 40 feet deep that is always at least half full of water.

_____ 4. The most formidable fighting man the world has ever known is the Apache Indian of the southwestern United States.

_____ 5. Performed regularly in Bangkok, Thai boxing allows the use of the feet as well as the fists and features the same weight divisions that are used in Western boxing.

_____ 6. Thai boxing tends to be much more rugged and dangerous than Western boxing.

_____ 7. In acupuncture and moxibustion, two ancient Chinese medical techniques that go back 2,500 years and are still practiced in China, needles are applied to nerve endings at 300 to 800 points on the human body.

_____ 8. Based on philosophies of nature and religion, these ancient forms of medicine could teach much to Western physicians.

_____ 9. Since automobiles are responsible for so much congestion and pollution, they should be banned from city streets.

_____ 10. Clarence Motherwell, a prominent psychiatrist, recently stated that "The reason most American men do little knitting is that, as children, they were taught that knitting was only for girls and sissies."

EXERCISE 28: *Do exactly as you did in the preceding exercise.*

_____ 1. Spiro Agnew has had many quarrels with the news media.

_____ 2. Since Chicano farm workers organized under the leadership of Cesar Chavez, their wages have gone up.

_____ 3. The future looks bright for Chicanos in California.

_____ 4. "Man has survived, hitherto, by virtue of ignorance and efficiency," Bertrand Russell has said. "He is a ferocious animal and there have always been powerful men who did all the harm they could."

_____ 5. The distance from Earth to the nearest fixed star has been computed at 25 million miles.

_____ 6. Says Arthur Schlesinger, Jr., "The common man has always regarded the great man with mixed feelings—resentment as well as admiration, hatred as well as love."

_____ 7. Man is a mere child in terms of the age of the world that surrounds him, and a day of unbelievable length extends before him.

_____ 8. The United States is a nation that has scarcely begun to recognize its potential for greatness.

_____ 9. By far the most dangerous land reptile in the world is the Australian tiger snake.

_____ 10. As little as 1/14,000 of an ounce of tiger snake venom (two milligrams) can cause swift death by lung paralysis.

EXERCISE 29: *Extract the facts from each of the following sentences and create your own sentence from these facts. First, cross out any word or phrase that is not factual. You may add a neutral word if it's needed to make sense out of what remains.*

Example:

Original: The guests on Al Sullivan's July 13 program were ~~beefy~~ Garson Caldwell, former Chicago Bear backfield ~~great~~, and ~~muckraker~~ Ralph Nader, who last year ~~ranted~~ against the automobile industry's carelessness in failing to install safety devices in cars.

Revision: On July 13, Al Sullivan's program featured Garson Caldwell, who once played in the Chicago Bear backfield, and Ralph Nader, who recently exposed the auto industry's negligence with regard to safety.

1. In a raging denunciation launched from the Beverly Hilton against "right-wing party policies," liberal Republican Congressman Richard Hanes blasted especially what he tagged "fear campaigns within the party" and "reactionary policies that advocate three steps backward for every step forward."

_____

_____

_____

2. In the Venetian Room of San Francisco's Fairmont Hotel last week, Wilma Peepgrass, plump and fiery Western States Secretary of the National Women's Temperance Union, lashed out bitterly against the national trend toward teen-age tippling, calling it "a sickening descent into bestiality and drunkenness."

88

_____

_____

_____

3. Suave Turkish diplomat Ahmed Bey preferred to remain cool last week toward a
U.S. pitch that the Dardanelles and the Bosporus be more heavily patrolled by allied
forces in the eastern Mediterranean.

_____

_____

_____

4. "So far management has had the situation wired their way. But things will be different after the next election," snickered Coley Bilgewell, muscleman chief of a local
union, at a raucous rally aimed at pumping up the assets of _The Timekeeper_, Bilgewell's union propaganda newspaper.

_____

_____

_____

EXERCISE 30: _Do exactly as you did in the preceding exercise._

1. Paunchy, pin-striped Raymond "Muley" Sammins became the segregationist governor of Louisiana after a four-month campaign that recalled Huey Long's grassroots
pitch of the 1930's.

_____

_____

_____

2. In Garden Grove, racist H. Milford Meadows addressed 550 fellow rightists of the
John Birch Society last night in an hour-long harangue against what at one point he
slyly called "bleeding heart economic relief policies in the state."

_____

_____

_____

3. For thirty minutes, the defense attorney grilled J. D. Jackson, beefy, florid Mus-
kaloosa County sheriff, whose corn-pone surface manner hides the brutality that
allegedly caused county jail prisoners to scream about conditions to Governor
Arkley J. Wright last May.

4. Ever since he sang to the FBI about underworld affairs last January, mobster Tony (Big Pinkie) Pingitore has been holed up in southern Wisconsin trying to shake the racketeers who once made him wealthy and now want him hit.

_____

_____

_____

5. In Buenos Aires, Costa Rican man-about-town Jorge Alvarez tipped off the press today that he and American cineminx Loretta LaMesa were going to be married, a move that insiders claim is a way for playboy Jorge to put down his ex-wife, British cinema queen Elaine Bevan.

_____

_____

_____

EXERCISE 31: *Develop your own paragraph from the facts provided in the following short article. Before you begin to write, answer the questions that follow the article. Be sure to use you own words in your writings.*

The Sea Devil

Some say the last great pirate met his end when Edward Teach (Blackbeard to history) was killed in a Virginia river battle in 1718. Others contend that the Age of Piracy didn't close until freebooter Jean Lafitte disappeared into the Caribbean with his treasure in 1821. But to a generation of schoolboys now reaching middle age, the most magnificent marauder of the seas was Count Felix Luckner of Kaiser Wilhelm's Imperial Navy. . . .

Luckner—or the Sea Devil as he came to be called—was the very model of a modern buccaneer. He sailed under the German naval ensign instead of the Jolly Roger, and his prisoners succumbed to champagne and his courtly charm instead of to cutlasses. In seven months of 1917, his three-masted windjammer sent fourteen Allied ships to the bottom with a romantic flair that amused rather than terrorized the southern sea lanes and made Luckner into a postwar hero on both sides of the Atlantic.

His strongest weapons were the benign profile of his vessel and the theatrical talent of his crew. At the helm of a captured American clipper rechristened the

Seeadler (Sea Eagle) and specially outfitted in Hamburg as a Norwegian cargo ship above decks but a German auxiliary cruiser below, Luckner would peacefully glide up to a French or British freighter signaling some innocuous nautical request like "Chronometer time, please." The captain would slow down, disarmed by the Norwegian flag at the *Seeadler*'s mast and the sight of a woman on deck (Scandinavian skippers often take their wives along on cruises, so Luckner assigned a boyish crew member to don wig and skirts when a victim was sighted). Then, with well-trained precision, German colors were run up, a section of the rail clattered down to reveal a single cannon, and signal flags broke out with the warning: "Heave to or I will fire."

After each capture, the stupefied enemy captain and crew were taken aboard the *Seeadler*, and their ship was quietly sunk. In most cases, however, it wasn't long before they could be counted among the war's most contented prisoners— or, as Luckner preferred to call them, "guests." The captured captain was escorted to a plush cabin in the "Captains' Club" where he joined the skippers of earlier catches. All prisoners had virtual run-of-the-ship, and French and British magazines and phonograph records had been laid in for their amusement. Luckner offered a prize of £10 and a bottle of champagne—he had acquired 2,300 cases of Veuve Cliquot from one of his prizes—to the first man to spot enemy ships, and soon even his "guests" were scrambling up the rigging to search the horizon.

Not a man was ever lost in any of the *Seeadler*'s engagements. When his guest quarters became packed with more than 400 Allied seamen, Luckner stopped a French barque bound for Brazil and put them aboard, gallantly paying them full wages for the time spent on his ship and toasting them with a final glass of champagne. Then he ducked around Cape Horn into the Pacific to elude the warships sure to be after him, sank a few American vessels south of Hawaii, and was finally wrecked by a tidal wave in the Society Islands. After 2,300 miles of island-hopping in an open boat, he was caught by the British in the Fiji Islands. He could have avoided capture by using force but disdained because he was not in uniform.

Luckner's early career matched his war exploits perfectly. He ran away from his aristocratic Dresden family when he was 13 and sailed as a cabin boy in a Russian full-rigger. Tumbling from one adventure to another around the world, he became a kangaroo hunter, beach-comber, Mexican soldier, prizefighter, wrestler, and a member of the Salvation Army. Finally he got a chance to study for a naval commission and was picked to command the *Seeadler* because no one else had his sailing experience.

Once the war was over, however, Luckner could never recapture the romance of his buccaneering days. On successive world tours he gave rousing accounts of his voyages and, in the '30s, tried some feeble propaganda for Hitler. In 1939, too old for active service and somewhat suspect by the Nazis, he retired to a hunting lodge in the Harz Mountains. But the old pirate's spirit never waned: in 1941 he wrote wistfully to his biographer Lowell Thomas, "My yacht *Sea Eagle* is berthed in Stettin waiting for new adventure."*

*"The Sea Devil," *Newsweek* (April 25, 1966). Copyright Newsweek, Inc. 1966, reprinted by permission.

1. List five or more adjectives that you think vividly describe Luckner's character or exploits.

_____

_____

2. Choose the *one* adjective you think has the best possibility for development with facts found in the above article and define that adjective.

_____

_____

3. Make that adjective the controlling idea of one of the following topic sentences: During the First World War, Count Felix Luckner _____

_____

Although buccaneers like Blackbeard and Henry Morgan established a tradition of violence, _____

_____

4. Make a list of specifics from the article that support your controlling idea. You might try composing a brief outline:

TS: _____

  I. _____

    A. _____

    B. _____

 II. _____

    A. _____

    B. _____

5. Using your fact sheet or outline, write a unified, coherent, factually supported paragraph of at least 130 words.

EXERCISE 32: *Read the article below and complete the exercises that follow it.*

The Italians have a word for it—graffiti, the anonymous one-line scrawlings found on fences, billboards, sidewalks and washroom walls. Usually graffiti has ranked one rung below limericks on the literary scale, but lately the messages have gained a new respectability. Playwright Edward Albee admits that an inscription in a Greenwich Village lavatory inspired the title for his "Who's Afraid of Virginia

Woolf?" After Yale University released a map indicating that the Vikings rather than Columbus discovered America, the *New York Times* chose a graffito from an Italian district in Boston for its quotation of the day: "Leif Ericsson is a Fink." Even the scholars have taken note of the washroom wit. In a new study entitled "What the Walls Say Today," two UCLA professors suggest that graffiti may offer a message of sorts about human nature.

For five months, psychiatrist Harvey Lomas and his associate Gershen Weltman scoured Los Angeles's bars, restaurants, bus stations, schools and even hospitals. Their report, read at a recent meeting of the American Psychiatric Association, concluded that people write graffiti to prove themselves ("This Is Tony's Turf"), to insult ("Hugh Hefner Is a Virgin"), to excite others sexually ("Marion: $25"), and to communicate an opinion ("Marvin Can't Relate to His Environment") or a bit of humor ("Judge Crater—Please Call Your Office Immediately").

Although slum buildings and automobile underpasses yielded the most graffiti, the investigators claim that the urge to make one's mark is common to all classes. Among good, law-abiding middle-class types it is expressed through what Lomas and Weltman call "commercial graffiti"—bumper stickers and buttons. And if one is rich enough, says Lomas, he simply has his name inscribed over the lobby entrance of a 40-story building instead of painting it on a fence.

In passing, the researchers discovered that the legendary "Kilroy" is being challenged by a new, equally mystifying figure—"Overby." Usually, Overby graffiti announces little more than "Overby Lives" or "Overby Rules" or, as a sign off the Pacific Coast Highway put it, "Overby Has a Heskinny in His Frebus." At times, however, Overby seems to represent the unknown hand that picks young grafficionados for the Army; in Los Angeles one roadside sign read "Down with the Draft—Overby Strikes Every 7 Hours."

Judging from the graffiti around southern California beaches, the biggest teenage hangups are psychedelics ("Take LSD and SEE") and the discovery that the world is not Disneyland ("Mary Poppins Is a Junkie"). . . . University of Chicago students have compiled an anthology of bromides from Western movies on a Lake Shore Drive underpass: "I Don't Need No Stinking Badge," "He's Not Dead—He's in the Hills—But He'll Be Back If We Need Him." Some of the most sophisticated graffiti appears on the walls of the men's room in Harvard's Lamont Library: "Reality Is a Crutch," "War Is Good Business—Invest Your Sons" and "God Isn't Dead—He Just Doesn't Want to Get Involved."

Public personalities, of course, draw a heavy share of wall commentary. The current favorites: . . . "Stamp Out Bert Parks"; "Ad Hoc Committee to Draft George Hamilton"; "Ronald Reagan Eats Peanut Butter". . . .

Lately, more and more grafficionados seem to get their kicks from commenting on the works of others. On a New York subway poster, for instance, the message "Jesus Saves" has inspired the reply "But Moses Invests." A graffito in a San Francisco bar proclaims "My Mother Made Me a Homosexual"; beneath, someone has written "If I Buy Her the Wool, Will She Make Me One Too?" But the last word in dialogues appears on the washroom wall in New York's White Horse Inn. Writer A has written "I Love Grils." Writer B has crossed this out and corrected, "It's Girls, Stupid—G-I-R-L-S." Under which Writer C has scrawled "What About Us Grils?"*

*"Washroom Wit," *Newsweek* (October 10, 1966). Copyright Newsweek, Inc. 1966, reprinted by permission.

1. In the article above, what seems to be the main idea?

_____

_____

_____

2. At what point in the article is this idea most obviously stated? State it in your own terms:

_____

_____

_____

3. In the second paragraph, the writer classifies the major reasons, according to recent research findings, that people write graffiti. Can you find some graffiti that indicate still *other* motives? Write a paragraph classifying the graffiti you find.

4. Can you also apply the author's main idea to buttons or to bumper stickers? What do the buttons or stickers say to you? Write a paragraph giving the reasons why people display the particular stickers that they do. What does the sticker say about the person who owns it? See the following lists:

Bumper Stickers

Suppose They Gave a War and Nobody Came?
Let It Be [Ecology]
The Majority Is Not Silent. The Government Is Deaf
Dirty Old Men Need Loving Too
Legalize Freedom
America. Love It or Leave It
America. Change It or Lose It
America I Love You
God Bless America
Vietnam. Love It or Leave It
Old Soliders Never Die. Young Ones Do
Chicken Little Was Right
Ban the Bra
Do Your Thing (but Not on Me)
I Didn't Raise My Boy to Be a Soldier
I Didn't Raise My Daughter to Be Bused
Motherhood
Share Love
Go Gay

Have a Nice Day
Have a Nice Nite
Legalize Pot
The Devil Made Me Do It
War Is Not Healthy for Children and Other Living Things
When Guns Are Outlawed Only Outlaws Will Have Guns
Off the Pigs
Pigs Is Beautiful
Pig Power
Your Local Policeman Is Armed and Dangerous
Have a Nice Eternity
Have You Found Your Jesus?
Keep Our Cities Clean. Eat a Pigeon
Relax Immigration Laws. The Indians Did
Custer Had It Coming
Drive Defensively. Buy a Tank
Help Prolong Wildlife. Throw a Party
Overpopulation Is a Time Bomb

Buttons

Try It, You'll Like It

Love Lets Us See How Beautiful the
World Is

Go Intercourse Thyself

Caution. Love Spreads Germs

U Turn Me On

Today Is the First Day of the Rest of
Your Life

What You See Is What You Get

Sex Makes You Come and Go

Sex Relieves Tension

Love Now, Pay Later

5. This article was written in 1966, and the lists were compiled in 1972. Can you compile a list of new and different graffiti that you have observed? Classify your list according to topics and write a paragraph of your own accounting for the graffiti you find.

EXERCISE 33: *Read the following paragraph; then complete the assignment based on it.*

(1) The messages contained in Harley-Davidson advertising brochures promise escape or play on the prospective buyer's ego by suggesting that he can greatly enhance his image simply by owning a Harley-Davidson motorcycle. (2) Harley's ad for the 65cc Leggero, for example, suggests that its machine is "Big enough and strong enough to carry you wherever the spirit moves you," a clear salute to the freedom and largeness of soul of the rider. (3) Moreover, the Leggero is, according to the manufacturer, "Your ticket out of a world you never made," an appeal that the young and disenchanted might respond to. (4) The message in Harley's ad for their larger Rapido lives up to the name of the machine. (5) "Savage aggressiveness in the open country" is what the Rapido features, perhaps for the genuinely aggressive or for those who can safely pretend they are while aboard a Rapido. (6) Harley's ad for their two Sportster 1,000 models promises therapy along with transportation in "machines that straighten it all out . . . on the street, the strip or in your mind." (7) Harley's big bike, the 1,200cc Electra Glide is "a machine great enough to meet the expectations of a special kind of man." (8) Of course, what is implied is that the reader is that "special kind of man." (9) After all, who wouldn't enjoy the distinctiveness conferred on him merely by owning the Electra Glide? (10) Judging from the ads, the cost of any of these vehicles is an investment in personal uniqueness, manliness, and aggressive individuality.

The writer of the above paragraph is responding to the message of the Harley brochures quite differently from the way the company probably hoped he would. He's making a judgment about the nature of the appeal projected by the ads, seeing that appeal as based on a kind of propaganda. This propaganda promises the buyer something *more* than simply a means of transportation: increased sexuality, personal charisma, aggressiveness, luxury, therapy.

Using magazines, newspapers, advertising brochures, TV ads, or a combination of any or all of these, write a paragraph analyzing the appeals used by advertisements for a certain kind of product. Pay special attention to the *name* of the product: "Toronado," "Barracuda," "Rapido." Below are some possibilities:

1. Automobiles
2. Pickup trucks
3. Household furnishings
4. Cosmetics

5. Pleasure boats
6. Sports equipment
7. Clothing

EXERCISE 34: **A.** *Using the* Time *article "Fortress California" on pages 78-79, write a paragraph in which you take a different approach from that taken by the writer of the paragraph on page 79. If you wish, you may use one of the following suggestions as the subject of your paragraph:*

1. The residents of protected communities are doing more to lock themselves in than others out.
2. Living in guarded communities can increase one's physical security while diminishing one's privacy and anonymity.
3. Make an imaginative future projection about the possible long-range effects of such communities on the lives of all of us.

If you have information about the subject that goes beyond that given in the article, you may use it as added documentation. Don't neglect to back your speculations with specific, concrete support.

B. *Write a paragraph based on the excerpt about Hugh Hefner on page 82. If you read* Playboy, *you may be able to add material by Hefner himself, which often appears in the magazine.*

5
Organization

Providing support in writing is one thing; organizing that support is quite another matter. You might have an excellent fund of specific details and still be frustrated about how to arrange them logically or to their best advantage. In the preceding chapter we touched on an aspect of organization in our discussion of the paragraph on security measures in exclusive communities, yet we haven't really discussed outlining, which is the best and most effective method for a student to organize his materials.

The sort of paragraph we've been concerned with so far doesn't require much preliminary arrangement. You've simply made the specifics relate to the controlling idea in some sort of sequence. But as you make the transition from paragraph to essay, you'll need to be aware of the basic structure common to both. It's our theory that if you can organize a first-rate paragraph, you can also organize a short essay. In fact, we think that many a solid student paragraph could possibly be expanded into a short essay, an opinion we'll try to support in the next chapter. What we're saying, then, is that if you can write a solid 150-word, factually supported paragraph that has unity, coherence, and good sentence structure, you can also write a short theme that has the same characteristics.

Outlining

In organizing a successful essay, you first need to outline the points you want to make and arrange them in order of importance. If you simply plunge in and try to handle too many ideas at once, you're likely to place small ideas where large ones belong and vice versa. But if you take time before you write to think about the relationships between ideas, you can save yourself some time and frustration. Actually, the outline can be likened to a tourist's guide, which aids you in arranging a rewarding trip. It gets you to the main points of interest without making unnecessary tours through the boondocks.

The proper form for an outline is indicated below. In our opinion, it's less confusing to place the thesis (or topic sentence, if you are making an outline for a single paragraph) and the conclusion *outside* the outline itself.

Thesis (or topic sentence): _____

I. _____		Primary Support
A. _____		Secondary
1. _____		Tertiary
2. _____		Tertiary
B. _____		Secondary
II. _____		Primary
A. _____		Secondary
B. _____		Secondary
1. _____		Tertiary
2. _____		Tertiary
C. _____		Secondary
1. _____		Tertiary
2. _____		Tertiary
III. _____		Primary
A. _____		Secondary
B. _____		Secondary

Conclusion: _____

The outline form is marked by various divisions, as shown above. The divisions labeled by roman numerals provide the major or principal support for the thesis or topic sentence. The capital letter categories provide secondary support for each of the primary divisions. This secondary support is in turn developed by tertiary support, labeled by arabic numerals. One could continue this process of division still further, but unless you are writing a term paper or a complex essay, to divide further might create confusion.

The structure of the outline represents the proper positioning of smaller ideas in relation to larger, more significant ones. The thesis or topic sentence contains the dominant idea—the large idea—and it is expressed in the form of a generalization. The primary support is also a generalization, but it is narrower and more focused than the thesis it supports. The secondary and tertiary support represent the specifics—the small ideas—that develop the larger thoughts. This last level is the "nuts and bolts" of the essay or paragraph. Thus, the outline demonstrates that old principle of subordination—proper thoughts in proper places—that we talked about earlier.

Classification

The outline also demonstrates the principle of *classification*, one of the most important concepts used in any thinking process. Classification is the process by which large bodies of information are divided into smaller related groups on the basis of some principle of categorizing. We might demonstrate the concept of classification as it operates in an outline with the following example. Suppose the student has decided to write a paper on Ernest Hemingway. Perhaps one paragraph would describe Hemingway's personal traits and would attempt to prove that Hemingway's personality was as vital as his art. The writer might begin by jotting down a series of facts he's accumulated through reading and research into the subject:

1. During spells in the fighting in France during the Second World War, correspondent Ernest Hemingway sometimes moved as far as sixty miles inside German lines to gather strategic information.
2. Any visitor who stopped at Hemingway's Cuban farm, *Finca Vigia*, was always lodged, fed, and invited to stay as long as he wished.
3. In a wry compliment to correspondent Ernie Pyle, Hemingway once called himself "Ernie Hemorrhoid, the poor man's Pyle."
4. In June 1918, near Fossalta, Italy, a badly injured Hemingway dragged his wounded Italian comrade-in-arms nearly a quarter of a mile under heavy Austrian fire in an attempt to save his life.
5. Hemingway once loaned a Devil's Island escapee enough money to help him get back on his feet.
6. After the Adjutant General's staff investigated him for "possible violation of . . . regulations for war correspondents," Hemingway told General Buck Lanham, "I'm going to have the Geneva Agreement tattooed on my backside in reverse, so I can read it with a mirror."
7. During combat in France in 1944, Hemingway carried two canteens, one filled with gin, the other with vermouth.

8. From 1942-44, Hemingway, in a 40-foot fishing boat, gathered and relayed information about German submarines off Cuba.
9. When the tab came for a round of drinks, Hemingway always grabbed it good-naturedly.
10. Hemingway was often quick to give time and advice to young writers seeking help.

The above list of facts, although interesting, hardly constitutes an organized body of information. The first task the writer has, then, is to organize and classify the facts—that is, divide them into appropriate categories.

In this instance, the various facts might best be organized into categories according to the characteristics they point to in the famous author. For example, sentences 1, 4, and 8 can be grouped as proof of Hemingway's *courage*. Sentences 2, 5, 9, and 10 point up his *generosity*, his willingness to share with others. Sentences 3 and 6 illustrate his *sense of humor*. Sentence 7 is difficult to fit into the writer's principle of classification, so it may be set aside. Perhaps it can be used later. The writer may now try a tentative outline, beginning with a topic sentence.

Topic Sentence: The Nobel Prize-winning author Ernest Hemingway had many memorable personal qualities.
  I. He was courageous.
   A. 1
   B. 4
   C. 8
 II. He was generous.
   A. 2
   B. 5
   C. 9
   D. 10
III. He had a sense of humor.
   A. 3
   B. 6
Conclusion: Surely, such traits do more to recall Hemingway as a man than as a famous artist.

The writer might have more specifics concerning Hemingway's personality, of course, and they could also be included. But if they were too numerous, the writer might have to distribute them over two paragraphs in order to ensure against excessive paragraph length. In essay writing, there is no law against writing two paragraphs on one aspect of a topic, provided that aspect is important.

As can be seen, the writer has classified Hemingway's personal traits into three equally important categories. Then he has subordinated each specific to its appropriate category. Failure to determine which are the major, or general, ideas and which are the minor, or specific, ideas can result in an outline like the following one, which fails to develop logically:

I. He was courageous.
   A. Tried to rescue wounded comrade.
   B. Constantly placed himself in dangerous situations.
II. He always picked up the tab for drinks.
   A. Would let people freeload at his farm.
   B. Helped down-and-outers with gifts of cash.
III. He had a sense of humor.
   A. Joked about himself.
   B. Laughed with soldiers over grim humor of war.

In the above outline, division II is not organized correctly. It is not properly coordinated with divisions I and III. It is a *specific fact*, whereas the other two primary categories are generalizations, as they should be. The statement that appears above as division II should therefore be placed in the category of secondary support and labeled with a capital letter. It illustrates the generalization that Hemingway was generous.

A few additional hints about the setup and wording of outlines may help to prevent errors. Teachers of writing generally agree that each category of an outline should have at least *two* divisions to ensure adequate development. Thus, if you have a roman numeral one, you must have a roman numeral two. If you have A under I, you must also include B. You may, of course, have more than two categories, but you should try for *at least* two.

Since the similar divisions of an outline are *coordinate* (of equal rank), they should also be grammatically coordinate. Below is an example of an outline in which the writer has failed to provide division headings that are grammatically parallel.

I. Courage
   A.
   B.
II. Generous and kind
   A.
   B.
III. He is funny.
   A.
   B.

Obviously, the first category heading is simply an abstract noun, which is perfectly acceptable. But division II, which should then also be an abstract noun, is stated instead as two adjectives. Division III is expressed still differently, as a short sentence. All three should be *coordinate* and *parallel* in their grammatical structure. One possibility might be as follows:

I. Hemingway's courage
II. His generosity
III. His humor

Another and perhaps better possibility:

Topic sentence: Ernest Hemingway had admirable personal traits.
  I. He was courageous.
     A. Tried to rescue wounded comrade.
     B. Scouted the enemy far behind the lines.
 II. He was generous.
     A. Always paid for drinks.
     B. Gave cash to down-and-outers.
III. He was funny.
     A. Joked about himself.
     B. Shared humor of war with military personnel.

Notice that the secondary supports are also grammatically coordinate and parallel in the above outline. The writer needn't follow the exact wording of the outline when he writes the essay itself, but he should follow the direction taken by his outline. If the outline has unity and its categories are grammatically coordinate, those characteristics ought to be reflected in the structure of his writing. If the writer takes the time in the outline to work out the relationships among ideas of varying degrees of importance, he will save himself valuable time in writing the final paragraph or essay. He will also be sure of a reasonable *singleness of purpose* in his writing. Another advantage of preparing an outline for your essay is that you can add to an outline if something important should occur to you after you begin to plan, and this will not necessitate rewriting the entire essay.

By this stage in your development as a planner and writer, you should be able to relax the rigid rule we made regarding the necessity for main clause unity. As long as each sentence (either in its independent or subordinate parts) contributes to the point of the paragraph, it could be said that singleness of purpose exists in the writing. You should also be able to make an outline of anything you intend to write. Outlining is the key to organization, both in the paragraph and in the essay.

Summary

1. The outline represents a method of dividing or classifying a large body of facts into smaller related ones.
2. The outline should be divided into primary categories, represented by roman numerals, and secondary categories, represented by capital letters. Further division is also possible and sometimes necessary.
3. The topic sentence and the conclusion should appear *outside* the outline.
4. The topic sentence represents large ideas; primary support represents medium-sized ideas; and secondary and tertiary support represents small ideas.
5. Equal categories of the outline should be worded in a grammatically parallel way; they must be *coordinate* in the outline, although the writer needn't follow the exact wording of the outline when he writes the finished paper.

EXERCISE 34: *Ideally, an outline represents a descent from general to specific. In each of the following groups, the statements range from very general to very specific. In the blank, write the letters in order of descent from the most general to the most specific.*

1. a. Last week a 32-year-old mechanic and mountain climber from Prague used an innovation of his own in rescuing three Frenchmen from the slopes of the Matterhorn.
   b. European mountaineers are a hardy and inventive breed.
   c. "Necessity," it has been said, "is the mother of invention."
   d. Adolph Zampach used a series of complex pulleys to hoist Jean Sembeau, Maurice LeBlanc, and the injured Gustave Bain from a ledge on the east wall of the Matterhorn.

Order of descent: _____

2. a. A 6-foot timber rattlesnake bit Frank Freeman on the right thumb, putting him in the hospital for a week.
   b. Snakes, especially venomous ones, must be dealt with carefully.
   c. Frank Freeman learned about venomous snakes in a painful way.

Order of descent: _____

3. a. Most people procrastinate when it comes to Christmas shopping.
   b. Stu Rubine suffered a fractured left arm when he was knocked down an escalator by a 200-pound woman who was in a hurry to get home.
   c. On Christmas Eve, Stu Rubine found Macy's to be as dangerous as combat.

Order of descent: _____

4. a. Nothing ventured, nothing gained is Frank's motto.
   b. To reach potential clients, salesman Frank Ginanni drives daily on Route 34, nicknamed "The Ambush" by local residents.
   c. In an average day, Frank Ginanni takes all kinds of risks to earn a living.

Order of descent: _____

5. a. While admiring a pretty pair of legs, Mel Milbaum stalled his rented Fiat on the Via Veneto, an event that led to a fist fight and Mel's arrest.
   b. When in Rome, do as the Romans do.
   c. For Melvin G. Milbaum, stalling his car on the Via Veneto led to the most embarrassing day of his life.

Order of descent: _____

6. a. *Anna Christie* was performed at the *Courtyard Playhouse* last weekend.
   b. New Yorkers claim that any earthly thing a man wants can be found in New York.

c. In the New York theater alone, a person may choose his entertainment from a wide variety of offerings.

Order of descent: _____

7. a. Philadelphia Superior Court Judge Elwood Webb today sentenced Emil Scopic to thirteen years in the state penitentiary.
   b. In recent years Superior Courts have been stiffening their attitude toward those who commit grand larceny.
   c. Cheaters never prosper.
   d. The court's sentence in embezzler Emil Scopic's case was unexpectedly severe.

Order of descent: _____

8. a. Bartley Maxwell's shares in several choice stocks rose dramatically last week.
   b. After being turned down on five successive occasions, Bartley Maxwell finally got a "yes" by revealing to his girlfriend that his shares in United Tinfoil had gained fifteen points in last Tuesday's market.
   c. Nothing succeeds like success.

Order of descent: _____

9. a. In Athens on Monday, fiery Greek actress Maria Poppolopoulos gained a divorce from American actor Stuart Dixon on the grounds of his unconventional behavior.
   b. Maria charged Stu with listening every night to rock music until she could no longer stand it.
   c. Greek "love goddess" Maria Poppolopoulos revealed recently that "American men make lousy husbands."

Order of descent: _____

10. a. Among Europeans, wine has a reputation for enhancing conversation.
    b. In a Budapest tavern, Tibor Laszlo did a lot of talking to the wrong person.
    c. In wine there is truth.
    d. Under the influence of a crisp Rhine wine, Soviet agent Tibor Laszlo made some significant revelations about an important dossier to a lady who turned out to be a British spy.

Order of descent: _____

EXERCISE 35: *This exercise will give you practice in preparing a topic outline for a paragraph. Rearrange the following items according to their logical order in the form of a topic outline, just as you would if you were outlining your own paragraph. The topic sentence and the concluding sentence are included in the details. Use your own paper to make your outline; designate the sentences by their number rather than by writing each one out, as shown in the following example.*

Example

1. On opening its doors, one Washington junior college had 12,000 students.
2. J.C. enrollment is impressive.
3. U.S. junior colleges are a growing concern.
4. Administrative needs also reflect growth potential.
5. J.C.'s will require 1,500 new academic deans by the 1980's.
6. "By the year 2000," says one dean, "the J.C. will be one of the nation's largest industries."
7. Five billion dollars will be allotted for J.C.'s in the next ten years.
8. In the next fifteen years, 1,400 new J.C. presidents will be needed.
9. Fifteen million dollars soon to be spent on one J.C. alone.
10. A million and a half students are currently enrolled in U.S. junior colleges.
11. In five years, junior college enrollment will increase by a million students.
12. Money allotted for J.C.'s is significant.

Topic sentence: 3
  I. 2
    A. 10
    B. 1
    C. 11
 II. 12
    A. 7
    B. 9
III. 4
    A. 8
    B. 5
Conclusion: 6

1.   1. Hippies experimenting with new family systems.
    2. Post offices employ many hippies.
    3. A few hippies secretly subsidized by parents.
    4. Hippies eat a lot of rice and cereals.
    5. Hippies establish their own social norms.
    6. Hippie family often resembles tribe.
    7. Says one San Francisco leader, "Let squares kill each other. We live, man, live!"
    8. Macrobiotic diet is popular with hippies.
    9. Sometimes as many as twenty people live together as a family.
  10. Some hippies earn their living by selling drugs.
  11. Macrobiotic diet is Buddhist in origin.
  12. Hippies think of family as a "cooperative."
  13. Hippies also have unusual means of support.
  14. Hippies even advocate special diets.
2.   1. Much of middle class migrating to the suburbs.
    2. Middle-income people migrate to find space.

3. Emphysema is now nation's number two killer.
4. Breathing New York City air for one day equivalent to smoking two packs of cigarettes.
5. Big city mayors have many problems in common.
6. People with low incomes fighting for decent schools.
7. Discontent of poor and dispossessed.
8. Two million middle-income whites have left cities.
9. To solve their problems, U.S. cities will have to have dynamic mayors.
10. Twenty-five thousand Chicago families on relief.
11. Air pollution is threat to health.
12. Highest incidence of lung cancer is in cities.
13. Deprived citizens strike for slum clearance.
14. Minority groups riot during summer months.

3.
1. Party representation mainly middle class.
2. Typical member fears for his job.
3. Members earn about $125 monthly.
4. Major motivation of NPD (German National Democrats) is fear.
5. These signs worry Western observers.
6. Most party members distrust other nations' influence.
7. Typical party member lives in suburbs.
8. Party's main objective is strong nationalism.
9. Party members desire return of Polish-held territory.
10. Desire end of American domination.
11. "The European Alliance threatens us," says one member.
12. One NPD man afraid he will lose his business.
13. NPD voter commutes to work.
14. Germany's NPD party extremely conservative.

4.
1. Wives expected to dress conservatively.
2. Although dedicated, corporation execs' wives say that corporation life has its trials.
3. Husbands must often travel excessively.
4. "Whenever the office calls, he has to go, even at 3 A.M.," says one wife.
5. All these demands make wife's role trying.
6. Corporation social life demands repressive conformity.
7. Wives discouraged from inviting "outsiders" to parties.
8. One exec logged 125,000 miles in nine months.
9. Corporation women expected to drink, but only "one or two."
10. One firm expects each exec to put in at least two hours a day on weekends.
11. Some firms expect wives to entertain once a month.
12. Some execs spend three weeks on the road for each week at home.
13. Corporation men must put company first in their lives.
14. One wife reportedly saw her husband a total of sixty days last year.
15. Wives expected to be "good listeners" but discreet.

EXERCISE 36: *Do exactly as you did in the preceding exercise.*

1. 1. Despite valiant efforts by local citizens, blob spread on Cornish beaches.
    2. Seamen on off-shore craft fought oil slick.
    3. Two thousand soldiers and Marines scoured rocks along coast.
    4. Military firefighting units also hit rocks with high-pressure hoses.
    5. English fought bitterly against oil spread that followed *Torrey Canyon* wreck.
    6. Women emptied boxes of detergents from piers.
    7. Thirty-six vessels treated waters off Cornwall with detergents.
    8. Even civilians on beach battled oil blob.
    9. Smaller craft dumped tons of detergent in shallows.
   10. Army helicopters carried detergents back and forth on beach.
   11. Little children tried to help with beach pails.
   12. Army and Marines also tried to stem oil flow.
2. 1. More than 70,000 factory chimneys in city.
    2. Overcrowding a major problem.
    3. Average dweller has only about 70 square feet of living space.
    4. Over 11 million people reside in city proper.
    5. About 200 traffic injuries occur each day.
    6. Ten thousand new vehicles registered each month in Tokyo.
    7. Policemen occasionally need oxygen inhalation.
    8. Air pollution rate is alarming.
    9. Tokyo in 1970's becoming an urban nightmare.
   10. Fifty-four public housing apartments drew 400,000 applicants in 1966.
   11. Increase in number of automobiles brings problems too.
   12. Forty tons of soot fall yearly on every square mile.
   13. Without a miracle, Tokyo will scarcely be habitable in future decades.
   14. To purchase car, Tokyo resident must have access to off-street parking.
3. 1. Agent functions as star's psychiatrist.
    2. Only superstars have a chance to survive without agent.
    3. Agent handles particulars for artist.
    4. Must keep client encouraged despite bad breaks.
    5. Show-biz agent performs indispensable services for client.
    6. Agents often handle legal details for client.
    7. Agent sometimes "soft-pedals" bad publicity.
    8. Agent bargains with studio over star's salary.
    9. Plans publicity campaigns.
   10. Agents have even been known to baby-sit.
   11. Choose appropriate names for clients to improve "image."
   12. Agent must help client rationalize failures.
4. 1. Many divorcees seek psychoanalysis.
    2. Some divorcees turn to liquor.
    3. Other wives, formerly friends, may distrust woman after she's divorced.

4. American divorcee pays for freedom in several distinct ways.
5. Yet despite shock of divorce, most women readjust.
6. Raising children multiplies problems.
7. Acquaintances of couple often loyal to ex-husband and reject ex-wife.
8. Wife has less money for support of family.
9. Suicide rate of divorcees three times that of married women.
10. Facing psychological repercussions is most difficult aspect of going through divorce.
11. Children miss male figure in household.
12. Losing some former friends inevitable.
13. Boys especially need father's help.

5. 1. Fifteen-foot makeshift craft became waterlogged, tangled in seaweed, nearly sank.
2. On Bathurst, they found themselves in "green, wet hell."
3. Finally landed on deserted side of Bathurst Island.
4. Tropical cyclone blasted them off course far from final destination.
5. "If we had not had each other, we would have died," said Bourdens.
6. Tiny kelp crabs attacked their wounded legs.
7. French couple named Bourdens fought desperately for survival.
8. "For days, the big wind and great seas drove us."
9. Lived on rainwater and sea snails.
10. Island jungle was practically uninhabitable.
11. Heavy seas swept yacht 500 miles off course across Timor Sea.
12. Attempted raft trip was even more hazardous than jungle.
13. Reptiles coiled together like worms in trees.
14. Crocodiles fought viciously within sight of couple.
15. Australian ship *Betty Jane* spotted raft four days off Bathurst and rescued couple.
16. The Bourdens' submerged legs began to ulcerate.

EXERCISE 37: *The following paragraphs are organized in a unified, logical way; organize a topic outline for each one. In composing your outline, divide the paragraph into primary, secondary, and, if necessary, tertiary support. Keep the topic sentence and the conclusion separate from the categories of the outline.*

1. (1) The differing expectations of two generations might be dramatized in a discussion between a grandfather and grandson over what traits distinguish an ideal college teacher. (2) On certain matters there would be no argument. (3) Like his grandfather in the post-World War I classroom, the collegian of the 1970's expects his teacher to have a thorough knowledge of his subject matter. (4) And today's sophomore would probably agree with Grandpa that the professor ought to be competent enough to publish at least a modicum of material in his field. (5) But while Grandfather would be willing to settle for that, his grandson expects a great deal

more. (6) Today's professor should be dynamic, a man with the ability to electrify a class with a brilliant lecture at each meeting. (7) The teacher should also be fair in his grading practices and before assigning final grades should always consider whether or not the student is making an effort. (8) In addition, the modern student expects the professor to show an awareness of problems existing outside the classroom. (9) But the trait that today's student seems to desire most in his teacher is enthusiasm, and a professor will be forgiven for a host of classroom sins if he displays that prized quality. (10) So while Grandpa appears to have accepted the eccentricities and sometimes the tyrannies of his professors without much complaint, his grandson insists that the student, too, has his rights.

2. (1) Discus-thrower Al Oerter had to overcome some serious obstacles to win his event in the 1968 Olympics. (2) According to many observers, Oerter's age was against him. (3) At thirty-two, he was supposedly past the age of peak capability, despite his own confidence in his capacity to improve. (4) One pessimist even suggested that Oerter's speed in the discus ring had been steadily diminishing over the past few years. (5) In addition, the pressing demands on his time kept him from devoting as much effort to his sport as he had in the past. (6) He is a supervisor for the Grumman Aircraft Corporation, a position that sometimes keeps him busy for ten hours a day. (7) Moreover, Oerter is a family man who enjoys spending a great deal of time with his wife and two children. (8) But Oerter's most serious handicaps are two persistent and painful ailments. (9) Since 1963 he has been the victim of a slipped cervical disc, a painful injury that necessitates his wearing a collar when throwing. (10) To add to his problems, he suffered a torn thigh muscle in an accident during a competition at Mexico City. (11) Working in a rain-soaked ring, Oerter slipped and fell during a trial throw. (12) In the finals, he had to numb his leg with ice in order to compete. (13) Despite all these difficulties, Oerter is optimistic about his future in athletics, saying, "I think I can continue to improve until I'm forty or so."

3. (1) From the teacher's point of view, the ideal student has a number of rare characteristics. (2) For one thing, he is eager. (3) That is, he needs little encouragement from the instructor to read 100-page assignments or to write 10-page documented papers. (4) An eager scholar gladly accepts difficult assignments with the conviction that they will help him to improve as an individual as well as a student. (5) He is also disciplined. (6) On any evening, this serious student can accomplish one or two hours of outside study for each hour spent in class. (7) He can sit at his desk for long periods of time, without needing the radio to entertain him or his friends to console him. (8) His most distinctive trait, however, is that he *likes* intellectual discourse. (9) He enjoys knocking ideas together to hear the sound made by the collision of, say, the views of Bertrand Russell and those of Pope Paul VI. (10) Such a person finds a classroom discussion of Spinoza or Wagner or Shelley as diverting as many other people find a good movie or a jam session. (11) He *wants* to discuss the political concepts of the Nixon Administration or the economic theories of John Maynard Keynes, and he never feels that such speculation is a waste of

time. (12) After all, the ideal student is an intellectual, a term once applied by Marya Mannes to anyone who enjoys and appreciates the play of his mind for the sake of that play alone.

4. (1) Since the invention of the tractor, an amazing variety of farm machines have been developed. (2) Some machinery is designed for highly specialized operations. (3) For example, there are now hay choppers and hay crushers as well as hay balers. (4) And advanced technology has led to the development of beet diggers as well as tomato-picking machines. (5) Huge "land-planes" for leveling the earth for irrigation are now commonplace in large agricultural areas, and one manufacturer is working on a machine for crushing rocks into a pulverized mixture that can be spread back over the soil. (6) On the other hand, some machines now perform several functions. (7) The small, all-purpose combine is good for 125 different crops. (8) In addition, the forage harvester can be used for both corn and hay. (9) Finally, a few radically different tillage tools have appeared, notably the rotary tiller invented by the Swiss in 1911, a machine that in one fast and violent operation can completely prepare rough land for seeding. (10) It goes without saying that twentieth-century farming is mechanized farming.

5. (1) In Sir Richard Burton, the adventurer, Victorian England produced one of the nineteenth century's most versatile men. (2) For one thing, Burton was an explorer. (3) In 1856, he fought fever and insects to become one of the first two Europeans to see Africa's Lake Tanganyika. (4) During this trip, Burton also stumbled upon the source of the Congo River, a fact he realized only years later. (5) His stature as an explorer was matched by his reputation as one of England's finest anthropologists. (6) In his examination of the forbidden Moslem cities of Mecca and Medina, Burton reported with great objectivity on the mores and customs he observed there, including the institution of polygamy. (7) His travels to remote cities on the Nile provided him with enough information on the erotic rituals of the East to later translate the tales from the *Arabian Nights.* (8) To his other talents Burton added an unparalleled mastery of languages. (9) He had at his command some thirty dialects from northern and central Africa. (10) These tongues ranged from Kanuri and Oji to Jolo. (11) Besides these, Burton spoke Arabic fluently enough to delight the king of Egypt at an Alexandria ball. (12) In his spare time, Burton also mastered at least six European languages, including French and Italian. (13) Such multiple talents, of course, made Burton a giant among Victorians and a biographer's dream.

6. (1) As the result of bitter experience, most girls will quickly recognize several types of dreadful dates. (2) The most common is the "Big I." (3) This fellow is a veteran braggart who doesn't waste a moment to begin thrilling his date with stories of his triumphs in sports, in business, or in bed. (4) He generally uses the girl as a "straight man" to feed him questions about himself, which he then proceeds to answer at great length. (5) Sometimes the Big I lets his lucky date look at his scrapbook or imagine how nice it would be to spend a lifetime listening to him talk about himself. (6) Even less attractive is the "Animal." (7) This guy deliberately tries to be crude on the assumption that the louder a man can belch at the table,

the more virile he is. (8) The Animal is famous for turning into an octopus at midnight—all arms. (9) If a girl somehow slips out of his grasp, he becomes very contemptuous of her, as if to say, "Stupid chick! You've missed the opportunity of a lifetime." (10) While the Animal is the most difficult to fend off, the "Tortoise" is the least so—he seldom threatens a girl with even a good time. (11) The Tortoise, like the creature he resembles, never utters a sound. (12) On a date with this creature, a girl is forced to carry the whole conversation while the Tortoise looks longingly at her as though he had thoughts that lay too deep for words. (13) Sometimes he doesn't even get past his date's home, preferring to drink beer with her father rather than risk the uncertainties of the social world. (14) Most self-respecting women would rather stay home and watch television than date one of these men.

EXERCISE 38: *Arrange the following details in a topic outline containing three roman numeral categories. We'll provide you with a start in devising the roman numeral headings.*

Thesis: Professor Bruno Schnorkel is one of the most eccentric people around.

1. Looks up at ceiling for five minutes at a time without acknowledging class.
2. Will yell at wayward student, "You couldn't find your rear end with both hands."
3. Owns an automobile that is, at best, obsolete.
4. Wears odd clothing.
5. Socks are often mismatched.
6. Picks up chalk at desk, walks to board as if to write, then puts down chalk and walks slowly back to lectern.
7. Often screams at slow student, "You'd be hard-put for an answer to hello!"
8. Lives in unique surroundings.
9. Drives a 1929 Auburn touring sedan with a black chassis.
10. Car has yellow fenders and green spoke-wheels.
11. Has large hooked nose, with tufts of hair protruding from nostrils.
12. Sports a wide polka-dot necktie and a tie clip in the form of an arrow, which is made to look as if it is piercing the tie.
13. Often seems absent-minded and forgetful in classroom.
14. Has out-of-the-ordinary looks.
15. Embarrasses students in class.
16. His houseboat residence has been run aground on the mud flats.
17. Cultivates a wild, bristling mustache.
18. Comes to class wearing a narrow-lapeled, gray flannel suit jacket over baggy brown gabardine pants supported by suspenders.
19. Lives in an old, abandoned houseboat.
20. Hair is cut like a West Point cadet's—sides and back of head shaven, top longer but standing up straight.
21. Wears a faded blue beret with egg stains on it.

Thesis: Professor Bruno Schnorkel is one of the most eccentric people around.

I. *Eccentricity of classroom behavior* _____

    A.

      1.

      2.

    B.

    and so on.

II. _____

III. _____

Conclusion: (Make up your own summarizing sentence for your essay.)

6

The Form of the One-Paragraph Essay

To prepare ourselves for the expansion of the one-paragraph paper into a complete essay—let's say a five-paragraph paper—we need to take another look at the form of the one-paragraph paper. Perhaps it may be easier for us to visualize this form if we give it an actual, physical structure. The topic sentence, of course, begins the structure. This is so because, as we saw in the paragraph on Dr. Malcolm in Chapter 1 (p. 2), the topic sentence contains the dominating idea of a paragraph. We also saw that the dominating idea is a generalization and that the ideas that develop or explain it are specific, concrete statements. Another way of expressing the relationship between the generalization and the specific statements is to say that the dominating idea is the big idea, or the broad idea, and that the specific statements are smaller or narrower ideas. We can then illustrate the relationship between general-big-broad and specific-small-narrow by actually giving a paragraph a spatial shape.

Each of the three statements in the structure is actually smaller or narrower than the generalization or the big idea in the topic sentence—not because we have put them in that particular position, but because each of them focuses on one of the three specific and concrete (or small, narrow) aspects making up the one general statement or big idea of the boring Dr. Malcolm.

Topic sentence (big idea)	A session in Dr. Malcolm's class is a boring experience.
1.	1. In a voice more soothing than a lullaby, Professor Malcolm reads page after page of factual information from the old black binder that holds his undergraduate notes.
2.	2. At some time these notes must have gotten mixed up, because there doesn't seem to be any pattern or organization to them, which makes it impossible to follow his lecture.
3.	3. Malcolm's voice is not only soothing, it's so singsong and monotonous that everything he says sounds the same, whether he's talking about Fort Knox, the British pound, the gold standard, or the theories of Ricardo.
4.	4. But maybe worst of all is the way he habitually looks away from his notes (I guess he memorized them fifty years ago) toward the far wall and then up to the ceiling, as if he were talking to God about Adam Smith and the gold standard.

If we look at the paragraph more critically we see that, although its shape approximates a T-square, this is not quite the shape that we want. Something is lacking; the T-square shape is right as far as it goes, but it ends too abruptly. And that, of course, is exactly the trouble; it is chopped off, truncated. Look at small idea number 4. You will immediately see that it is not an ending, a conclusion; it's merely one more small idea, and there is no real reason for stopping the paragraph at this point, other than that the writer simply ran out of gas. But that is not a good enough reason. Your paper should end only when you have provided sufficient support to validate the big idea, thereby satisfying the reader's curiosity and laying his doubts to rest. The end must always be accompanied by a signal to the reader that you think you have done these things and that you are now winding it up. Your conclusion rounds off the whole paragraph and completes its form. It is the last of the three basic parts—beginning, middle, and end.

Fortunately, most of us have an inborn sense of form, and at the very least, a lack of form or a distortion of it makes us feel uneasy. We want books, stories, essays, jokes, and even one-paragraph papers to have form. If you pay attention to the twinge of uneasiness that you feel when you see something unfinished or formless (shapeless), you should be able to recognize formlessness even in your own writing.

Now to return to Dr. Malcolm. Since we have already expressed the controlling idea in our topic sentence, we have our *beginning*, and because we have expressed our small ideas in specific statements, we have our *middle*, and the hardest work is over. What remains to be done—to add a conclusion or an *end*—is a relatively simple matter. All we must do now—and essentially this is how all conclusions are arrived at—is sum up, recapitulate the small ideas to recall the reader's attention to our big idea. We must echo the big idea, restate it, say simply in one way or another, "and now because of what I have shown you in my small ideas, you can see the validity of my big idea—how boring Professor Malcolm's economics class is." Naturally, we are not going to say it in quite these words, but we will say something that adds up to that. Sir James Jeans ends his classic essay in which he tells us why the sky is blue with a brief summary of the body of his paper and the statement "That is why the sky is blue."

By now, perhaps, you are beginning to guess that if a paragraph with a beginning and a middle is shaped like a T, then a paragraph with a beginning, a middle, and an end will be a T crossed at the bottom as well as at the top (a double-crossed T)—or an I, or the cross section of an I-beam, whichever you prefer.

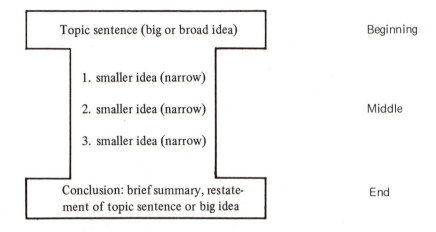

Topic sentence (big or broad idea)	Beginning
1. smaller idea (narrow)	
2. smaller idea (narrow)	Middle
3. smaller idea (narrow)	
Conclusion: brief summary, restatement of topic sentence or big idea	End

And now to fill in the bottom cross piece. Since the paragraph is not very long, you could perhaps merely say:

Wow! Is Old Professor Malcolm ever boring.

You might, however, wish to sum up the specific ideas with a more formal ending:

Certainly, Ricardo and Adam Smith would be bad enough by themselves, but with Old Malcolm and his singsong voice, his out-of-date notes, his humorless and incoherent delivery, topped off by his crummy eye contact [and now you restate your controlling idea] —well, if you want to commit suicide slowly, come into Dr. Malcolm's class and be bored to death.

Another variation might go something like this:

So any way you look at it, there's no contact in this class. The students don't know what Professor Malcolm is talking about, and Professor Malcolm doesn't care that they don't know. To spend an hour at the mercy of a teacher who years ago stopped caring whether or not he got through to his students is my idea of the most boring experience in the world.

In this example, you might have noticed that we don't repeat any of the small ideas in summing up the middle or body of the paragraph; yet observe that the first two sentences in effect do sum up their thoughts. Often this is sufficient, provided you repeat, in some manner, as the last sentence does, the big idea (controlling idea) of the topic sentence. A brief, indirect reference to the small ideas may suffice, as implied by the "Wow!" above, which deftly suggests all the small ideas and recalls them to the reader's mind. You might also have noticed that "Wow!" serves as a bridge from the small ideas across to the rest of the statement, which echoes the big idea.

Often, a conclusion may briefly summarize the small ideas and echo the big ideas without referring directly to them:

"Quit gripin', man," the voter advised. "That guy Doolin's a swinger."

Notice how deftly the word *swinger* includes all the details (the small ideas) of easy money, free trips abroad, beating legal raps.

Deft, yes. We could do well to take as our motto for the composition of conclusions "the defter, the better." But not all of us can be deft—at least, not all the time. Certainly, as compared with "Wow! Is Old Professor Malcolm ever boring" and "That guy Doolin's a swinger," our slower and stiffer *hence*'s, *therefore*'s, *so you see*'s, *so*'s, and *in short*'s seem stodgy. However, any ending that does the job of recalling to the reader both our small ideas and our big idea so that the reader knows beyond any doubt what we have been talking about will usually suffice. We should remember that a simple ending, good enough for Sir James Jeans, is probably good enough for us, most of the time: "That is why the sky is blue." It's simple and it works. It would make for a dull conclusion only if you had nothing to say in the first place.

We can see, then, that it doesn't make much difference how we organize our conclusion, as long as we have one and as long as it accomplishes two jobs—summarizing the small ideas and restating the big idea—both of which are an unmistakable signal to the reader that the paragraph is ending. We can also see that, aside from completing the meaning of the paragraph, the conclusion helps to satisfy our esthetic sense, of which our sense of form is a part. What is shapeless or truncated (unfinished) offends us. What is complete and well formed pleases us, and a piece of writing has the power to please through its form as much as any physical object does. Hence, even in a one-paragraph paper—the shortest and simplest piece one can write—we should always keep in mind the importance not only of the meaning, but of the form as well. In a piece of writing, meaning and form blend into each other and become indistinguishable. It is only to study what makes a piece of writing work that we separate the form from the meaning. Usually they work together, each heightening, each perfecting the other—if we let them.

To help us appreciate the importance of form in its relationship to meaning, let's turn once more to old Malcolm and put just the bare bones of the ideas into our I-shaped paragraph. Notice that there are small ideas that follow each of the numbered ideas. What category of items in the outlines in Chapter 5 do these correspond to?

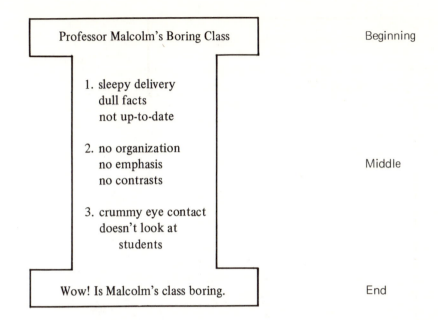

The advantage of placing a paragraph inside a diagram for practice is that it helps us to visualize the difference in size of the various thoughts and parts of a paragraph or essay. Most of us need to see with our eyes in order to "see" with our minds. Hence, to have a diagram before our eyes helps us to place ideas in their appropriate relationship.

Summary: Form

1. The big idea or generalization or dominating idea is a part of your beginning or your introduction. It crosses the T at the top. It begins the form.
2. The small ideas or the specific, concrete statements that develop your big ideas make up the column of the T or I. Often three of them are just about right. This makes up the middle part, or body, of the paragraph or essay.
3. The brief reference to your small ideas and the restating of your big idea—the summing up—widens your paper out again to make the bar that crosses the T at the bottom and completes the I. This is the ending or conclusion. It rounds off and completes your form.
4. Remember:

BEGINNING

Middle
Middle
Middle

END

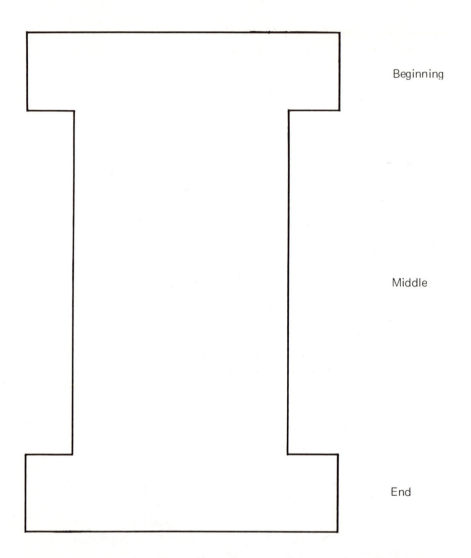

Beginning

Middle

End

EXERCISE 39: *In the I-shaped space above, place in the appropriate positions the items from your topic outline of one of the paragraphs in Exercise 37.*

The resemblance between outlining and placing the topic ideas of a paragraph in an I-shaped figure probably had occurred to you before you did this exercise. Now, of course, the resemblance is quite plain. However, seeing the topics inside a spatial shape may help you to better understand the principles of outlining. Placing topics inside an I-shape might serve as a substitute for outlining. Whatever you think about this, just remember that any kind of technique or device that you use is worthwhile if it helps you to understand the relationship between form and meaning and if it thereby enables you to write better than you did before.

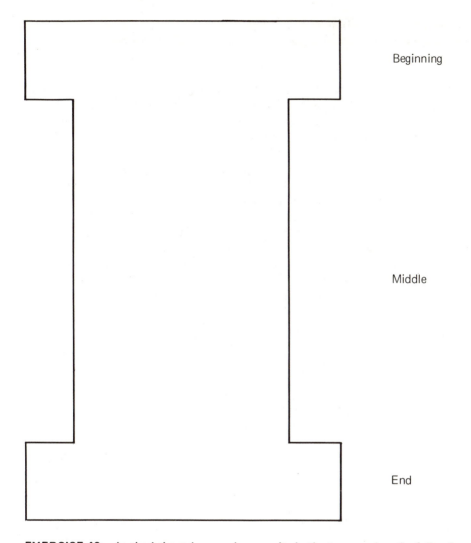

Beginning

Middle

End

EXERCISE 40: *In the I-shaped space above, write in the top crossbar the following topic sentence: "Each of Olaf Torgerson's three children resembles him in some way." In the column (middle part) of the diagram write down a few brief ideas that show these resemblances and number them 1, 2, and 3.*

Example: 1. *Trygg has his father's powerful but graceful build.*
2. *Peter has his father's craggy but thoughtful face.*
3. *Looie has his father's strong but sensitive hands.*

Then, in the bottom crossbar write a conclusion.

Example: *By build, face, and hands, each shares something of Olaf Torgerson. Some part of the man is reborn in each son.*

119

You may, of course, make the children boys or girls and give them any names you like; and of course take any tone you please—serious, humorous, or whatever.

EXERCISE 41: *On your own paper, make and label an I-shaped diagram. Then write in the diagram a paragraph of about 150 words based on the Olaf Torgerson topic sentence. Make sure your paragraph has a beginning, middle, and end. Remember, for children you may substitute either girls or boys or make any other changes that might be more suitable for whatever you want to say about the Torgersons. A word of caution: form and the classification of ideas into big, little, or otherwise are not substitutes for thought. The awareness and use of form and organization will help you to think; they will not replace thinking. The variety of things you can say about Olaf and his three children is almost infinite; but don't get carried away. Remember that the qualities in the offspring that you are tracing to their father must make some kind of sense, if not on a serious level, then at least on a humorous one. So don't forget to use your common sense.*

7
The Form
of the Essay

You are probably beginning to protest that not all one-paragraph papers are shaped like a T crossed at top and bottom or like an I. You are right, of course. Some one-paragraph papers are shaped like an inverted T ($\perp$), with a bar at the bottom and none at the top. Others have nothing at top or bottom, but rather have a bar—or at least a bulge—somewhere in the middle ($+$). (Some have no shape at all; but, as you have found out, they don't work very well.) At any rate, these other forms can work just as well as our T-shape, but unless you are an experienced writer, they are much more difficult to use.

After all, it is logical that the topic sentence should come first. Remember, your big idea is the guide. You look to it for direction. Everything you say must follow the line of thought introduced in the topic sentence. You cannot stray from the path of the subject of the big idea. Each of your small ideas develops the big idea by being about or related to it. Also, with your topic sentence as the first sentence of your paragraph, it is easy to check to see if such a relationship actually exists. For example, if the big idea in your topic sentence is the thrill of body contact in football, you must talk about the particular thrill, not about some other one. But since it is so easy and pleasant to let our thoughts stray, we might find ourselves three-fourths of the way through our paper putting down something like this: "And then I'll never forget the fun of just being part of the gang in that old football squad at Union High." By now, if you have really tried to improve your writing, you have probably discovered that straying from the subject is easy. But you have also found out that with the topic sentence at the beginning, all you have to do to see that you're on the right track is simply to look back to that sentence and there it is, as plain as day. Being one of the gang on the squad may have been fun, but it isn't related closely enough to the kind of thrill described in your main idea. So cut it out of the paragraph; it doesn't belong. There is nothing wrong with it as an idea—but not for a paragraph about the thrill of body contact in football. This thought brings us to another and quite different kind of advantage in getting the main idea down at the beginning.

As we swing into the activity of writing down our small ideas to develop our big idea, we often run into difficulty for three basic reasons: (1) we are not interested enough in our subject; (2) we don't have enough information to develop our subject; (3) other ideas related to but not subordinate to the big idea keep forcing their way into our paper.

The solution to the first problem, lack of sufficient interest, is obvious: change your topic to fit what comes into your head most easily—that is, whatever you are really interested in. If instead of the thrill of body contact, you keep recalling the bus ride home late at night with all the guys singing, then throw out the old topic and use the new one, the pleasures of being one of the gang.

In dealing with the second problem, lack of information, you have to be honest with yourself and admit that you didn't really have any right to choose that subject in the first place—simply because you didn't know enough about it. Instead, choose something that you have enough knowledge of to write about. If you still hanker after your original big idea and have a hunch that it is a good one, that can be taken care of by your going to the library and getting the information you need to back up and develop your big ideas.

The solution to the third problem is what this chapter is mainly about. First, however, we must clearly identify the problem. Often, an idea of equal importance to your big idea keeps cropping up, if not in your paper at least in your mind. You want to talk about both the fun of being part of the squad and the fun or satisfaction of achieving something either as an individual or as part of a team, whether in tennis, football, basketball, track, baseball, water polo, or whatever. Or maybe what had started out as a paper having as its main topic the misery of playing second fiddle to an older brother has turned into a paper on the combined miseries of being caught in the middle between Big Brother and Little Sister with Mom and Dad thrown in for good measure—the wealth of ideas and details depending on the depth and scope of your miseries. Then the more you look at these various gripes or miseries and really think about them, the more examples and incidents supporting and illustrating these ideas begin to crowd into your head. Put them all down on your paper where you can see them and keep going, listing all the things that bug you—Brother, Sister, Mom and Dad, car insurance, job, school, and the whole catastrophe. Then, if you are a serious student—that is, more interested in improving your writing than in expressing your miseries—you will realize at some point that your one-paragraph paper has become an impossibly crowded mess. So be it. Don't be alarmed. What has happened is that in your attempt to develop your big idea through specific and concrete statements, every detail you have written down has led you to recall several other related details. It seems as if everything has conspired to make you turn out ideas. What you now have is enough material to expand your one paragraph into five paragraphs.

The main difference between the one- and the five-paragraph paper is one of scale; the overall form is the same. A five-paragraph paper stands in relation to a one-paragraph paper much as a heavyweight fighter stands in relation to a flyweight fighter: there is simply more to the big one.

Before we examine the mechanics of expansion, however, let's look at a student's one-paragraph paper that he later expands into a five-paragraph essay. Here is the paper in its original, one-paragraph form:

Although I agree that sports are important to students, I believe that the experiences a man has later in life are much more important to him than those of playing in the "big game."

    1. One of the greatest of experiences in life is marriage. Here a young man is tested in ways and to a degree that he'll never encounter in a football game. If a young man and his wife are really in love with each other, they'll have a unity and teamwork superior to any football squad's.

    2. Many valuable experiences also occur when a man begins to earn a living. He soon learns the ups and downs of life as he enters into a competition that is tougher than any sport and that is played for higher stakes. If he made too many mistakes in a game, no one suffered very much, but now, if he is fired for making too many mistakes at his job, his whole family may suffer great privation.

    3. Then in his declining years a man has the joy not only of his children but of his children's children and of growing old together with his wife.

So you see, the experiences of playing in the big game cannot compare in importance with the experiences a man has later on in his life.

Beginning

Middle

End

We don't necessarily see what the writer wants us to see in his paragraph. Part of the trouble is that the subject is too big to be developed convincingly in one paragraph or in a mere 190 words. His three small ideas in the column of the I, though smaller than his major idea, are still too large and too general, lacking the concrete specific detail that convinces us that the writer knows what he is talking about. The second sentence in item 2, for example, is better, mainly because it begins to develop the first statement. But there isn't enough of this kind of material to make the paragraph work, and even the "ups-and-downs" statement is too general and undeveloped; there simply isn't

123

enough room in such a short paper to provide the necessary specific detail to develop so many general statements. Because the writer was getting his ideas down, he was lulled into thinking that he was writing convincingly. But he wasn't—he was only including generalizations instead of giving specific examples that would illustrate the general statements.

The student, however, does have the fundamentals of a good essay. He has the skeleton, an outline of his ideas that he can expand into a multiparagraph paper. He has five basic items: the beginning, the three middle items, and the end—five things finite and definite enough for him to focus on. He can make the expansion without any desperate floundering if he keeps in mind the relationship between the flyweight and the heavyweight fighters and one- and five-paragraph papers. The following essay, representing the student's expansion of the one-paragraph paper, is the student's reply to an essay entitled "In Defense of the Fullback" by sportswriter Dan Wakefield.

In Defense of Life

Beginning

1. I agree with Dan Wakefield in his standing up for sports in his essay "In Defense of the Fullback." However, I find myself opposed to his main idea that nothing we experience later on in life can compare in importance with our sports experiences in school. The expression used in describing the so-called glory was the fullback's "eighty-yard run," and the author makes it stand for the highest achievement in the athlete's life. Supposedly, he will never again do anything else so great, and thus the rest of his life will seem very dull. I feel that just the normal living of life contains many experiences far greater than that of the "eighty-yard run."

Middle

2. One of the greatest of all experiences of life is marriage. Here a young man is tested in ways and to a degree that he would never encounter in a football game. If a young man and his wife are really in love with each other, they'll have a unity and teamwork superior to any football squad's. The loyalty a man owes his wife is based on a closer human relationship than the loyalty a boy owes the other members of a football team. Raising children also brings with it experiences of all types. Looking at the children and knowing they are yours and that you must take care of them and raise them is a lot more challenging—and should be more satisfying—than four years of looking at the other members of the team on the field and around the campus. Many men look at this time when their children are young and completely dependent on them as the most cherished period of their lives. When Tad Jones (the Yale coach quoted in the Wakefield essay) made the statement that "the big game was the most important moment in a player's life," he must have been forgetting the pride a father feels when he sees his son or daughter graduate from high school or when he admires a portrait of his family. Certainly, experiencing marriage and family life is at least as thrilling as playing in the "big game."

3. Many valuable experiences also occur when a man begins to earn a living. He learns the "ups and downs" of life and begins to realize what competition really is when he starts working for keeps instead of playing for fun. This is part of the struggle of life, and the stakes are his family's welfare and his sense of his own worth. He learns the joy of doing a job well and being paid for it. As he progresses in his job, he begins to experience the sense of his own value in the contribution that he makes to the world. Gradually he sees that his experience in sports was child's play in comparison with the events of his working career.

4. Another time when we experience many wonderful things is in our declining years. During this time we often become aware of the beauties of life. The falling of early snow or the sweet freshness of a spring day may be very dear to an aging man. A man and his wife growing old together share many fulfilling experiences, such as spending time not only with their own children, but with their children's children.

5. Thinking, then, of the variety and seriousness of the experiences a man has throughout the course of marriage, work, and parenthood, you may agree with me that "eighty-yard runs" and playing in big games are insignificant child's play in comparison with the experiences of mature life.

Though the student has not been entirely successful in his expansion, this is obviously a much better paper than the one-paragraph paper. It is important to note that the faults of the longer paper are not due to its expansion. That was pretty easy: the student used the same form and simply enlarged it and subdivided its ideas to discuss them in more depth and detail. Rather, the faults of the longer paper are caused by the same sort of carelessness that was responsible for the faults in the one-paragraph paper. But notice that because of the clarity of form in the longer paper, no less than in the shorter paper (beginning, middle, end), the faults can easily be seen; we can isolate them and set to work eliminating them.

The errors and faults in the essay should be apparent to you, and you should be able to identify most of them. There are mechanical errors. The essay does not adhere to the principles of coherence and organization and subordination that we have already discussed. One of the paragraphs is better than the others. Throughout the essay the student fails to provide enough specific and concrete detail for the central idea. Nevertheless, there are some strengths in the essay—an important one being the writer's enthusiasm, which always helps make an idea interesting. In the main, the essay has unity, continuity, and emphasis—all deriving from its form. It is the form that provides the structure for both the original one-paragraph essay and the expanded five-paragraph paper.

Remember first of all that a longer paper has essentially the same structure as a one-paragraph paper. Each has a beginning, a middle, and an end. Look at the essay on pages 124-25 and note the labels we have added. The first paragraph is the beginning;

the second, third, and fourth paragraphs all belong to the middle or body of the paper; and the fifth paragraph is the end. To help you see this more clearly we'll put a skeleton of the five-paragraph paper into the familiar I-shape in which we first placed the student's one-paragraph paper. Thus, we have the following diagram:

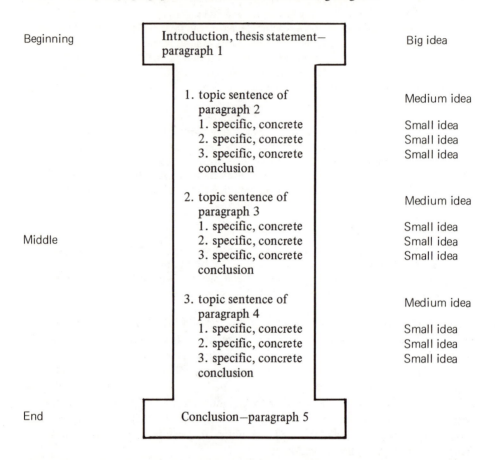

| Beginning | Introduction, thesis statement—paragraph 1 | Big idea |

1. topic sentence of paragraph 2 — Medium idea
   1. specific, concrete — Small idea
   2. specific, concrete — Small idea
   3. specific, concrete — Small idea
   conclusion

2. topic sentence of paragraph 3 — Medium idea
   1. specific, concrete — Small idea
   2. specific, concrete — Small idea
   3. specific, concrete — Small idea
   conclusion

3. topic sentence of paragraph 4 — Medium idea
   1. specific, concrete — Small idea
   2. specific, concrete — Small idea
   3. specific, concrete — Small idea
   conclusion

Middle

End — Conclusion—paragraph 5

Now what we have done is put the opening paragraph in the crossbar at the top of the I. This first paragraph serves as the introduction to the paper, but at the same time it also contains the main idea of the whole paper, and because of this we call it the *thesis statement*—that is, the statement that represents the controlling idea of the entire paper. (Remember, in your one-paragraph papers the topic sentence was the controlling idea.)

Next, we put the student's second, third, and fourth paragraphs in the column of the I, the narrow part. These three paragraphs develop the paper's thesis just as the small ideas in a one-paragraph paper develop its topic sentence, and in both cases they make up the middle part or body of the paper. Keep in mind that each of these three middle paragraphs is shaped exactly like the entire paragraph of a one-paragraph paper. Remember also that each one has a topic sentence with its main idea stated at the top or beginning of the paragraph. Additionally, each has three (more or less) small ideas, which we show on the diagram as "specific, concrete." (Actually, in the student's essay, every paragraph but one has its own conclusion at the bottom. Which one does not? How does the lack of a conclusion weaken the paragraph?)

There is, however, one very simple but important difference. The big idea in the topic sentence of each of these middle paragraphs is the big idea only in its own paragraph. It is not the biggest idea of the whole paper; it has now become subordinate to the big idea in the thesis statement in the first or introductory paragraph. Because it is smaller than the thesis-statement big idea but larger than the smaller, supporting ideas in its own paragraph, we call it a *medium idea*. This should be clear to you if you study the diagram on page 126.

The small ideas in the one-paragraph paper have moved up to become the topic sentences (medium ideas) of the three middle paragraphs, while the big idea of the topic sentence of the one-paragraph paper has become the big idea or thesis statement of the whole paper. This new form, the five-paragraph paper, is what we call the *one-three-nine* form.

One stands for the big idea in the thesis; *three* stands for the three medium ideas in the topic sentences of the three middle paragraphs; and *nine* stands for the total number of the specific and concrete, or small, ideas that we have in each of the three middle paragraphs. It might help us to understand the relations among these thirteen ideas and to grasp the significance of their various functions in contributing to the sense and form of the entire essay if we think of them as a family unit. Think of the *one* as a grandfather, of the *three* as his three children, of the *nine* as the three children of each of the first children—grandchildren of the old man. The first three children are equal to each other and subordinate to, or smaller than, their parent though directly related to him. The grandchildren are all equal to each other and subordinate to, or smaller than, their respective parents; although directly related to their parents, they are only indirectly related to their grandfather. Keep in mind that of the thirteen, Grandfather is boss; he was the original big idea, and without his existence, none of the other twelve would have come into being. A similar relationship exists among the big, the medium, and the small ideas in our five-paragraph paper.

To help you get a mental image of the overall shape of a five-paragraph paper as well as of the individual paragraphs within it, especially the middle ones, we will draw an outline of the five paragraphs inside the form of the entire essay.

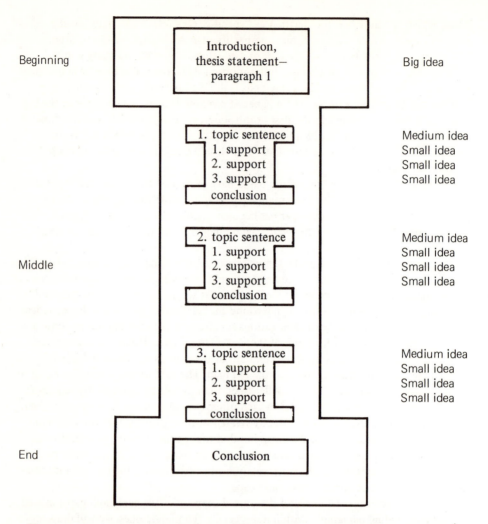

| Beginning | Introduction, thesis statement— paragraph 1 | Big idea |

	1. topic sentence	Medium idea
	1. support	Small idea
	2. support	Small idea
	3. support	Small idea
	conclusion	

Middle	2. topic sentence	Medium idea
	1. support	Small idea
	2. support	Small idea
	3. support	Small idea
	conclusion	

	3. topic sentence	Medium idea
	1. support	Small idea
	2. support	Small idea
	3. support	Small idea
	conclusion	

| End | Conclusion | |

The next step is to examine the forms of the individual paragraphs in the student's essay. The first paragraph is diagramed on page 129.

Both the first and the last paragraphs are in the shapes of plain rectangles to suggest openness and a variety of possible shapes. We are not much concerned here with beginnings and endings for their own sakes. In the "beginning" paragraph, we recommend that your thesis statement be at the end with introductory material preceding it. We prefer this for two reasons. First, you need some sort of background material to lead your reader up to the thesis statement—to show him how you got there, as in the following introductory paragraph. You need somehow to get him interested in what you are going to be writing about. Second, placed at the bottom of your opening paragraph, the thesis statement is followed by the topic sentence of your first middle paragraph, which begins the development of the thesis. Conclusions you are already familiar with. Writing a conclusion for a five-paragraph paper is essentially the same as writing one for a one-paragraph paper. In concluding the one-paragraph paper you sum up less

> I agree with Dan Wakefield in his standing up for sports in his essay "In Defense of the Fullback." However, I find myself opposed to his main idea that nothing we experience later on in life can compare in importance with our sports experiences in school. The expression used in describing the so-called glory was the fullback's "eighty-yard run," and the author makes it stand for the highest achievement in the athlete's life. Supposedly, he will never again do anything else so great, and thus the rest of his life will seem very dull. I feel that just the normal living of life contains many experiences far greater than that of the "eighty-yard run."

Big idea or thesis statement.

important ideas contained in the body of the paragraph; in concluding the longer paper you sum up the medium ideas, which are expressed in the topic sentences of each of your middle paragraphs.

Because all the middle paragraphs have the same shape and labels, we will diagram and discuss only the first middle paragraph of the student's paper. Remember that what we say about the first middle paragraph applies to all middle paragraphs in our system. A diagram of paragraph 2 from "In Defense of Life" appears on page 130.

Read paragraph 2 carefully. Notice how, by the simple act of diagraming the paragraph and by labeling its components, its faults and weaknesses are brought out into the open. You undoubtedly have many more ideas for improving this paragraph now than you did after reading it as it appeared in the essay. Is *marriage* the best word to use in the topic sentence? Should it, perhaps, be changed to *marriage and family life,* or *marriage and children?* Is the space devoted to the three small ideas uneven? Should the third small idea be lifted out of the Tad Jones sentence and be given more development and support by more specific illustrations of children's accomplishments? Or is the whole idea of children large enough to be made into a separate paragraph, distinct from the idea of marriage? Or, within the scope of the paragraph as written—except for enlarging further on the idea of children's accomplishments—is there a possibility of slightly altering the Tad Jones sentence and using it as a part of the concluding sentence (the summing up)?

One of the greatest of all experiences of life is marriage.

BEGINNING
Medium idea or topic sentence

Here a young man is tested in ways and to a degree that he would never encounter in a football game. If a young man and his wife are really in love with each other, they'll have a unity and teamwork superior to any football squad's. The loyalty a man owes his wife is based on a closer human relationship than the loyalty a boy owes the other members of a football team. Raising children also brings with it experiences of all types. Looking at the children and knowing they are yours and that you must take care of them and raise them is a lot more challenging—and should be more satisfying—than four years of looking at the other members of the team on the field and around the campus. Many men look at this time when their children are young and completely dependent on them as the most cherished period of their lives. When Tad Jones (the Yale coach quoted in Wakefield's essay) made the statement that the "big game was the most important moment in a player's life," he must have been forgetting the pride a father feels when he sees his son graduate from high school or when he admires a portrait of his family.

Certainly, experiencing marriage and family is at least as thrilling as playing in the "big game."

Small idea 1:
love between husband and wife

Small idea 2:
joys of fatherhood

MIDDLE

Small idea 3:
joys in children's accomplishments

Conclusion
END

One-three-nine. It's a strong, tightly knit form, and we think it will improve your writing. You have undoubtedly begun to wonder, however, if every essay must be exactly one-three-nine and why use one-three-nine in the first place. In answer to your first question: certainly not! An essay can have any number of paragraphs it needs to make its point. It will have, however, only one thesis, just as your school has only one president. But the number of middle paragraphs may vary from essay to essay. A short essay (any essay under roughly 1,000 words) may have two, three, four, or maybe even five middle paragraphs, depending on the paper's length and complexity. Each of these middle paragraphs may have two, three, four, five, or more small ideas supported by dozens of smaller ideas. In answer to the second question: we chose three and nine mainly because a 500- or 600-word paper usually requires about three medium ideas to support the thesis and three smaller ideas to support each medium idea. As a matter of fact, the number three turns up so often in so many quantitative, spatial, and logical relations that many people have attributed to it religious, mystical, and even magical properties. We don't need to believe in magic, however, to see that usually three reasons, three examples, or three illustrations will provide more support than two—although often two will suffice. On the other hand, it is usually superfluous to cite more than three examples or illustrations to support a single unified idea. Three is usually just about right. Consider, however, the one-three-nine relationship as only a suggestion for the structure of your paper, and don't be afraid to vary the three and the nine to suit your needs in a given paper. The one-three-nine form is meant to give you a sense of proportion in the structure of your paper, not to strait-jacket you.

Summary: Form of the Multiparagraph Paper

1. The need for the multiparagraph paper arises when our main idea has several related but parallel and equal parts that can be classified under one large topic.
2. Attempting to impose form on a smaller, one-paragraph paper or trying to organize what are often at first only a few tentative ideas helps us structure the larger paper. This is so because in our search for form we begin to focus on finite, specific concepts—something definite enough for our minds to "see" and begin thinking about. It is this process that releases a stream of thought with a sufficient quantity of ideas to make up a larger paper. This is what an Anglo-Saxon poet called "unlocking the word hoard."
3. For our purposes, we have assumed the multiparagraph paper to be an essay of about five paragraphs. The first paragraph is an introduction containing a thesis usually placed at or close to the end of the paragraph. The second, third, and fourth paragraphs make up the middle part, or body, of the essay. They develop the thesis. The main idea in each of the middle paragraphs is in the topic sentence, located at the beginning of the paragraph. Since these main ideas are smaller than the big idea controlling the entire paper yet larger than the small ideas beneath them, we call these ideas *medium* ideas. The fifth paragraph is the conclusion, in which we sum up the middle ideas and restate the thesis.
4. The overall shape of the five-paragraph paper is an I, the same shape as the one-paragraph paper. The three middle paragraphs also have this shape; they are simply smaller versions of it. The introductory and concluding paragraphs have a rectangular shape to suggest the relative *width* or the general nature of the ideas contained in them as compared with the width of those in the middle paragraph.
5. "One-three" is an arithmetical description of the one-paragraph paper. "One-three-nine" describes the five-paragraph paper.

EXERCISE 42: *Analyze the middle paragraph outlined in the diagram on page 130 in light of the questions asked on page 129. Rewrite the paragraph, incorporating the suggestions below.*

1. Improve the wording of the big idea to make it correspond more closely to the paragraph's development.
2. Develop the second and third small ideas in more detail to give them emphasis equal to that given the first small idea.
3. Eliminate some of the generalizations in the development of the first small idea and replace them with more specific, concrete details for examples and illustrations.
4. Make the Tad Jones statement part of the conclusion and improve the existing concluding statement.

EXERCISE 43: *Diagram the third paragraph found on page 125 according to the one-three-nine form. After you have done this, study it carefully; then rewrite it, making whatever alterations are necessary to improve it.*

EXERCISE 44: *Expand your one-paragraph paper on Olaf Torgerson (p. 120) into a one-three-nine essay, containing about 500 or 600 words in five paragraphs—the introduction or beginning rectangular, the three middle paragraphs I-shaped, and the fifth and final (conclusion or ending) rectangular. Consult the diagrams and explanations in Chapters 6 and 7, as well as the discussions of development in earlier chapters. This exercise will test what you have learned this semester about writing.*

EXERCISE 45: *Write a one-three-nine paper of at least 600 words on the subject of life's satisfactions. This is partly the topic of the essay "In Defense of Life"; but we are not asking you to take that student's point of view or to defend any of his arguments. Parts of his essay may help to bring your own feelings and thoughts to the surface, but your essay should discuss the aspects of life that you believe are the most worthwhile for you and that give you the greatest satisfaction. The subject of a paper is not the same thing as the big idea. It is a larger, more general concept from which we derive the thesis statement and big idea. As you can see from the examples below, the thesis statement and the big idea are distinct from, although related to, the subject. The thesis statement is more limited in scope than the subject of the paper; the big idea is the most important part of the thesis statement: it is the part that will be developed in the rest of the paper. In Example 1, the big idea is satisfactions from relations with other people. The writer's job is to show in what ways these relations are satisfying. In Example 2, the big idea is the writer's satisfying his curiosity about the future. The last sentence of this example is an example of a transitional sentence: it suggests the direction that the rest of the paper is going to take.*

1. Example: *Subject*   Satisfactions in life.
Thesis statement   "As for me, my main satisfaction in life comes from my relations with the people around me at home, at school, and at work."

2. Example: *Subject*   Satisfactions in life.
Thesis statement   "One of my main pleasures in life is satisfying my curiosity about the future—my own future, the futures of members of my family and of friends, the future of the world. For me, the unfolding of these futures is like watching a movie or reading a book."

3. Example: *Subject*   Satisfactions in life.
Thesis statement   "My most satisfying experiences in life take the form of various kinds of physical activity."

EXERCISE 46:   *Write a one-three-nine paper of about 500 or 600 words describing the three main steps in a process such as making a dress, tuning up an automobile engine, building a cabin, getting good grades in college, or making a pair of sandals.*

EXERCISE 47:   *Make another visit to Olaf Torgerson's family and describe a project the family has completed or an adventure they have shared. Show how each of the three children makes a unique contribution to the experience through some inherent or learned quality he has received from Olaf.*